Strategic Engagement

Strategic Engagement

Practical Tools to Raise Morale and Increase Results

Volume II: System-Wide Activities

Chris Crosby

Edited by Gary Gesell

BUSINESS EXPERT PRESS

Strategic Engagement: Practical Tools to Raise Morale and Increase Results
Volume II: System-Wide Activities
Copyright © Business Expert Press, LLC, 2019.

First published in 2019 by
Business Expert Press, LLC
222 East 46th Street, New York, NY 10017
www.businessexpertpress.com

ISBN-13: 978-1-94897-698-5 (paperback)
ISBN-13: 978-1-94897-699-2 (e-book)

Business Expert Press Strategic Management Collection

Collection ISSN: 2150-9611 (print)
Collection ISSN: 2150-9646 (electronic)

Cover and interior design by S4Carlisle Publishing Services Private Ltd., Chennai, India
Graphics created by Chris Crosby with special contributions from Celeste Crosby

First edition: 2019

10 9 8 7 6 5 4 3 2 1

Printed in the United States of America

To John, Robert, Gilmore, Merlyn, Celeste, and Gary.
Thank you for your love and support!

~

Special thanks to Ronald Lippitt, Richard Walton, Kurt
Lewin, John Wallen, and Richard Schmuck. Without your
foundational work, Robert P Crosby may not have had
the tools to synthesize this rich collection of activities.

~

Tremendous gratitude to Robert P Crosby: my father,
trainer, and mentor throughout my career. These volumes
highlight his ability to design and deliver strategic activities
to solve problems. They provide a definitive list of
his designs, which generated unheard-of business results,
the core second-year curriculum of his unique corporate
graduate program, and more.

Abstract

Strategic Engagement continues in Volume II with four more activities. In contrast to Volume I, I learned these activities after graduate school while working internally as an Organization Development practitioner under the mentorship of Robert P Crosby.

Volume II focuses on system-wide activities and includes group-to-group conflict, goal alignment, process improvement, and project or major initiative.

Combine this set of system-wide activities with what you learned in Volume I (conflict resolution between two employees or a boss and employee, work team development, and transition sessions) and you have a basic toolkit to transform any workplace culture.

Keywords

alignment; business results; change; change management; project; cross-functional; leadership; MBA; organization development; organizational development; productivity; project management; Stanford; team; work-group; workplace

Advanced Quotes for *Strategic Engagement Practical Tools to Raise Morale and Increase Results Volume II: System-Wide Activities*

"Chris Crosby has followed up his insightful first book, *Strategic Organizational Alignment: Authority, Power, Results*, with a well-written and well-organized sequel that expands upon the territory he illuminates in the aforementioned book and explores new and promising horizons. Crosby's two-volume book, ***Strategic Engagement,*** highlights eight practical core OD interventions that are needed today more than ever. This book is engaging, compelling, and replete with practical knowledge and wisdom."

—William L. Weis, PhD, Professor of Management, Albers School of Business and Economics, Seattle University

"Treehouse has benefitted from the pragmatic strategies presented in Strategic Engagement. Working directly with Chris Crosby while developing a team of facilitators capable of delivering many of these interventions in-house, Treehouse has gained alignment, reduced tension, and improved our plans for major initiatives. Facilitated conversations between individual employees, managers, and employees and groups within the organization have enhanced communication. As a non-profit, we are resource constrained and benefit from the efficiencies gained through this work. I highly recommend this book!"

—Janis Avery, CEO, Treehouse

"Chris has done a remarkable thing here. He has packaged the very tools he used to help me transform multiple workplaces in a way that is accessible and usable for all. These books are invaluable."

—Behzad Suroosh, Regional VP Supply Chain Americas, Beiersdorf AG

"If you really want to change and improve your company, then you must read this book! Chris lays out a strategy based on actual experiences that created demonstrable enhancements in a variety of environments, including my own companies."

—Clive Copsey, Global Director of New Product Development Alcoa

"Chris Crosby has provided us with a virtual outline for a graduate-level program in OD!

Amazing work, Chris!"

— Dr. John J. Scherer, Director, Scherer Leadership International Co-Creator, the Original LIOS MA-ABS Program Author, *Wiser at Work: Five Questions that Change Everything*

"*Strategic Engagement* (Volumes 1 and 2) offers practical and powerful tools to address critical challenges facing teams and organizations. The books address several important focus areas, including Conflict, Goal Alignment, Process Improvement, Transition Meetings, and Work Group Development. Chris has done a fantastic job of making it simple, easy to understand, and implement. An important book for all OD practitioners and consultants, it will provide ready access to critical interventions applicable for teams and organizations."
—Ragland Thomas, Vice President—Global Organization Development
& Strategy, Institute of Organization Development

"I have an extensive collection of business books, and this one is a real gem. I started my last two CEO positions with transition sessions as outlined in this collection and led by Chris himself. The activities in this book are the very activities I have used to lead to record results. I find it a remarkable collection and written in a way that is easy to comprehend and immediately effective."
—Brian Bauerbach, President & CEO, Mold Rite Plastics

"An immensely practical book packed with knowledge and wisdom to help people create efficient and effective organizations that get results. Chris has expertly synthesized and organized what can be an overwhelming amount of information and conceptual material into an easy-to-understand guide. Not only is this book tremendously helpful for professionals, managers and executives should read it with no less reverence than they would read their company's financial report."
—Ethan Schutz, President & CEO, The Schutz Company

"*Strategic Engagement* (Volumes 1 and 2) provides practitioners and leaders clear ways to improve productivity. The book blends theory with practice and allows organizations to create productive and engaged workplaces. Through step-by-step instruction, Crosby shows you how to navigate group-to-group conflict, articulate and align goals, and improve both processes and project initiatives. A must read for anyone in the field."
—Rodney D. Coates, Professor, Global and Intercultural Studies,
Miami University of Ohio

"An exceptionally clear and comprehensive two-volume book with relevant in-depth theories, practical steps, and specific tools to accomplish your goals.
A 'must read' for every leader and consultant."
—Brenda Kerr Minno, President, the Leadership Institute of Seattle

"This book is a great 'pocket book'—it's a leader's best friend—saturated with a road map that puts theory into action.

An organization is a 'network of relationships'. Crosby takes this maxim seriously, highlighting the many ways this network of relationships can fumble while providing clear steps for upgrading the entire system. Too many books give glamour to theory while missing the link of how theory is implemented.

I believe his book offers a bonus—the practice associated with this book not only leads to better results, but will lead to greater joy within the 'network of relationships' in the workplace. What a great bonus for such a great book."

—Timothy Weber, PhD, Licensed Clinical Psychologist

"The chapter called software basics is the blueprint of our change management strategy when we implemented a division global ERP system. Our roll-out was a success due to that strategy led by Chris. Many companies can have a successful technical ERP solution, but without the end users and business leader aligned and fully informed of the benefits and risk you can't have a successful ERP roll-out. It took everyone on the team to make our ERP implementation a success, but Chris's work on educating the business leaders and making sure the process owner's voices were heard about benefits and risk elevated our implementation from good to excellent."

—Mark Howard, Hawaii Operational Manager, Serta/Simmons

Contents

Appendices

List of Figures

Introduction

Strategic Engagement Volume II has six chapters and nine appendices. Chapters 2, 3, 4, and 5 represent core activities that solve specific system-wide organizational issues. The appendices add critical components to those chapters but can also be used as needed in various situations. For instance, Appendix E provides a practical brainstorming sequence that can be used in whole or in part as an alternative to how discussion topics are generated in Volume I for transition sessions or work team development. The sequence in Appendix E provides a simple and efficient way to reduce a large list to a manageable amount of actionable items, while gaining feedback from those who created the list.

I do not repeat any chapters but I repeat one appendix in Volume II, What Is a goal. This is because, ironically, I find many managers skip the hard work to ensure their goals are measurable. Yet, a core ingredient to create an engagement culture is measurable goals. Measurable goals are the seeds of engagement by which employees can grow and improve the workplace.

Volume II focuses on system-wide activities and includes how to *build implementation competency* and *break dysfunctional workplace silos.* There is a tried-and-true set of "socio-technical" components that must be used to ensure effective implementations. Chapter 1, Implementation Competency outlines such socio-technical components and they are integrated throughout both volumes of *Strategic Engagement.* Chapters 2, 3, 4, and 5 include a short section on breaking silos related to the activity you just learned. The complete series on breaking silos, coupled with the work learned from *Strategic Organizational Alignment (SOA),* provides the reader with a guide to success.

This book integrates the work of Robert P Crosby and my years of Organization Development experience. Many of the activities presented are scattered throughout the books *Strategic Organizational Alignment; Walking the Empowerment Tightrope; Cultural Change in Organizations (CCIO); The Cross-Functional Workplace; Fight, Flight, Freeze (FFF);* and

Leadership Can Be Learned. The rest are from experiences throughout my career.

Beyond the people already mentioned, many great minds deserve credit for this book's foundation, including, but not limited to, Dr. Timothy Weber, Dr. John Scherer, Dr. L.B. Sharp, Dr. Murray Bowen, Dr. Edwin Friedman, Dr. Carl Whitaker, Dr. Salvadore Minuchin, Gilmore Crosby, John Hanlen, Dr. Jay Hall, Dr. Ron Short, and Dr. Edgar Schein.

Who is the audience?

This book is written for those in organizations seeing the connection between increased engagement and results yet needing a little more direction to get it right. It is for the CEO, the manager, the project manager, the organization development consultant, and others trying to engage those around them more profoundly. It is a must for functions that constantly lead groups trying to solve problems such as Quality, Safety, Maintenance, Human Resources, Engineering, or for external consultants.

Volume II Book Layout

Part One—Implementation Competency. Chapter 1 reframes implementations and challenges the reader to increase their standards. Beyond words, I provide concepts and tools that are often neglected when organizations try new things or have settled for the ordinary. The concepts are integrated throughout my books and the entire two-volume set.

Part Two—System-Wide Implementations. Chapter 2, Group-to-Group Conflict provides a way to manage two or more groups either in conflict or struggling to support each other with the inputs needed to be successful. Chapter 3, Goal Alignment gives a step-by-step group process to align your organization to its goals. Chapter 4, Process Improvement shows how to use the employees doing the work to improve processes that run across departments. Chapter 5, Major Project or Initiative is a detailed way to lead a planning session to ensure a clear path to successful implementation. Chapter 6 gives the basics of software implementation that relate to all change in organizations.

The appendices contain the theories and extras needed to lead each activity. They are presented how I give them during sessions, including the actual words at each step of the presentation, rather than an in-depth theory analysis. Each theory is simple, practical, powerful, and intuitive; meant to frame sessions; and aid in group reflection, awareness, and interaction. My objective is to provide you the tools to be successful in presenting a range of theories.

Volume II is an extension of Volume I. Therefore, it is all new except Appendix D, What Is a Goal. Volume I has an extended lead-in that includes a preface, a section on engagement that explains its relationship to business results, and a section on how to use the volumes. Volume I, Chapter 1 highlights each activity, and Chapter 2, Strategies for Engagement provides a way to view engagement through systems thinking. Beyond that, Volume I has two chapters on facilitation: Facilitator Basics and The Facilitator Triangle. They are core to my practice.

Finally, a prerequisite for any facilitator is reading my first book, *Strategic Organizational Alignment*. It demonstrates how authority works within systems and a systemic diagnostic tool that identifies the sponsorship scenario needed to build an effective strategy in any situation. These two core frames help facilitators effectively lead any group session.

Volume II focuses on system-wide implementations. In contrast, the four activities in Volume I of *Strategic Engagement* are two forms of third-party conflict (boss–employee and employee–employee), transition meetings, and work team development.

♦♦♦

Section One
Implementation Competency

♦♦♦

CHAPTER 1

Implementation Competency

Many workplaces struggle with implementing a quality product on schedule. If you listen to the news, you hear all kinds of excuses for failed, late, overbudget, or subpar implementations. Building implementation competency is critical to success in today's fast-paced environment. This chapter includes a set of socio-technical components to increase implementation competency.

Introduction

Even great managers seem comfortable with less productivity when starting new ventures, such as building a new location, creating a new department, developing a new type of software program, or executing a major project.

Poor people-processes and implementation structures lead to poor results, rather than the belief that "we are going to have poor results because we are starting something new."

To illustrate, let me share a recent scenario. A dear friend of mine was having stomach problems. He thought it was because he was getting old. At 86 that seems like a logical reason. After all, the body does break down. But what if the reason was wrong? What if it was not about age at all? Or, at least not mostly. After an assessment from a naturopath and a simple regimen followed with discipline, his stomach issues vanished almost completely.

Implementation Competency Strategies

The same principle applies to almost all new scenarios.

"We are starting a new plant, so we will have bad production while we get the bugs worked out."

"This department's first efforts to do R&D are going to have many problems as they sort out how to do things."

"The first few months after we implement Oracle, expect delays as we fix the problems learned at go-live."

"This merger will take quite some time to iron out the details."

The above assumed outcomes have a few things in common. One, they are all real statements.

Two, the assumed outcomes can be, *mostly*, avoided.

What? Avoided? How?

They can be avoided in several ways.

Expectation Setting: If you set a low bar, you will get a low bar. Set it higher, but then follow up with a thorough, well-resourced, and calmly driven strategy.

People-process Strategy: Understand the difference between operation at startup and operation at maturity, and establish people-processes that quickly identify and resolve emerging issues.

Effective Temporary Governing Body: Create a simple decision process with the leaders over the areas where the new startup is happening. Apply this process to make quick decisions about emerging issues that impact the employees.

Manage the Ramp-up: Ensure an effective process is in place to raise and resolve emerging issues quickly in all impacted areas. That means identifying the future state and engaging with those who will use the new item. It is not good enough to only focus on a project team or the technical solutions. Rather, teach all new aspects to the end users before using it on a daily basis. Make sure you do this with ample time to fix issues.

Consequently, you will better understand potential startup issues and be more prepared to solve them as they arise. In the software industry these are your end users, but all other projects, mergers, or creations have internal customers who will use the products. Include them during ramp-up. It is not rocket science, yet that type of inclusion rarely happens.

Align the Managers over Impacted Areas: Alignment is not a one-time information session; rather it requires an ongoing people-process. What do managers need to know? Certainly they need to know when, what, and how the rollout will happen. But don't get confused. It is what change agents need to learn that matters. Change agents need to learn 1) how to effectively engage with each manager, 2) what issues the managers think will likely emerge, and 3) the managers' thoughts on the specific needs of the employees. That knowledge builds by collaboration throughout the process, and occurs in gradual steps while preparing for day one of the implementation. Fully aligned and engaged managers greatly increase workplace readiness, while decreasing the possibility of a go-live surprise.

Communication and Understanding Calms the Amygdala: The Amygdala is the small almond-shaped part of your limbic brain that is responsible for fear. During change it is on high alert. This is not just some touchy-feely voodoo; it is real and confirmed by the latest neuroscience. Expect fear and do not overreact. Also, the Amygdala is calmed by conversations and understanding. If you hold tight to any data until you know everything, then you add unneeded stress in your organization. Instead, communicate often, and then listen, learn, and appropriately respond to what you are hearing.

Do not accept poor results because something is new. Instead, use the following *socio-technical* concepts and create a strategy that significantly changes how you start new things.

- SPA: Single point of accountability on all mission-critical tasks or roles.
- By-When: Clear dates to complete tasks, and expectations to communicate if they slip.
- Follow-up process: Ongoing check-in to ensure actions and commitments are being completed and solving the original problem.
- Feedback process during ramp-up phase: Use a feedback process with the users of the product, process, or where the machine or new item will be implemented to raise emerging issues and concerns. Chart the issues visually and solve the majority of them quickly and efficiently.

- Effective governance: Use a decision process that balances the end-user needs, managers of the end users, and key business leaders with the project team.
- Align managers: Create and conduct a process to align and significantly involve or inform all managers over impacted areas.
- Align cross-functions: Align, clarify, and ensure input and communication to all cross-functional support groups.
- Effective resource management: Ensure the right and enough resources are available at new plant startups or at go-live during implementations, and that they remain until business results are stable. If you are a large corporation and allow a plant to start up without extra technical help, then you are managing too passively. Once you reach process stability, then adjust technical resources to normal operating levels. Do not start up a plant or implement a software system that runs your business with the same amount of resources as a mature operation or you risk poor results.
- Decision clarity: Balance manager authority and employee influence, and avoid any movement toward an extreme such as consensus.
- Startup or go-live process: Check in daily on what is working and not working and quickly solve emerging issues.

Does this list sound easy? Think again. One reason so many tasks and actions fail is the lack of personal authority to impose a structure that is effective (see pp. 75 and 218 of *SOA*). This is not a one-time shot. It is about follow-up, appropriate reprimands, positive reinforcement, being open to suggestions, and making minor tweaks until running well.

To save money in the long term, you must spend more money up-front. The trick is to be smart and not shortsighted. Implementation competency is a skill that is sorely lacking in most organizations. Organizations get more excited about new ideas than implementing them. Don't lose that excitement, but gain a better understanding, focus, and enthusiasm of how to implement.

After all, how much would Boeing have earned if they had reduced the startup problems of the Dreamliner in half? Maybe that sounds lofty, yet surely some reduction could have been achieved. One problem that successful businesses face is that they make so much money because of their position in the market that they can afford to be ineffective in their implementation competency. What is remembered is the sales after implementation, not the prolonged problems because of poor people and whole system processes. In fact, many blame departments and new processes for problems rather than having the courage to look at themselves, their (in)ability to align around change, and then applying effective implementation practices.

Conclusion

Many companies accept poor numbers at startups, mergers, software implementations, new R&D departments, and projects. Instead, apply effective implementation practices and adjust them until you achieve results. Set higher expectations and bolder goals; then deploy effective implementation practices to improve the result. Once you do that, you will gain a significant competitive advantage.

◆◆◆

Section Two
System–Wide Implementations

◆◆◆

CHAPTER 2

Group-to-Group Conflict

Almost all workplaces are interconnected, whether they recognize it or not. Yet most spend little or no time aligning, maintaining, and improving the connections to ensure effective cross-work relationships. Nor do many have continuing conversations to ensure each group has what they need, when they need it, to be successful. Most groups depend on others to provide the materials, information, tools, and resources to do their jobs. Rarely are all inputs to one's job self-contained within their group.

Introduction

This chapter provides a step-by-step process to improve the working relationship between two or more groups. Most workgroups must interrelate with other workgroups for results. Those interactions often do not work well and sometimes cause work task disruption. However, these interactions can almost always be improved.

What follows is a straightforward, repeatable way to raise the issues and problems and implement solutions and structures to create a better functioning organization.

To succeed, strong sponsorship is required from the leaders over the struggling departments. Herein often lies the problem. Whether aware or not, many managers do not have cross-group connections on their radar and some inadvertently stop their employees from improving situations by creating rigid boundaries with whom they can and cannot interact.

Change this dynamic by adding positive cross-group interactions and consistent follow-up to improve results. The proper platform and engagement structure helps your employees realize their full power to influence situations by stating what is needed to be successful and ensuring they are heard.

This chapter describes how to manage cross-group conflicts or situations where task disruption, information sharing, and basic work processes are not working well. It is presented in the following scenarios. First, a simple *group-to-group* improvement like an order entry group to a warehouse. Second, between *multiple groups* that must coordinate to support a core group such as production. Finally, *silos* where *two or more groups are deeply entrenched* and not working well together.

Preparation

Preparation for cross-group work is critical. This type of work can have multiple managers that may or may not report up to the same boss. Depending on the organization's size, you may have to go several layers to find an Initiating Sponsor. Therefore, the Sustaining Sponsors are key for the cross-group work to be successful—meaning they must come together to clarify goals and provide ongoing sponsorship to ensure the actions are followed up until meaningful results are consistently achieved.

Cross-group work normally begins with three possible scenarios. A boss that manages several groups that are not achieving desired results may ask for help to increase productivity. Or, two or more managers of groups that must work together may request assistance. Another possible scenario is that a manager recognizes the need to improve their group's interfaces with other groups, and advocates to their superiors and peers. **Prepare the Boss(es):** In each case, learn about the boss's goals and help sharpen them as needed (see Appendix D, What Is a Goal). Cross-group work may involve several processes. Each process can have measurable goals to improve. If measurable goals are not known, then help the bosses generate clear goals before the session.

Beyond the goals, review the meeting agenda and explain each stage. Help the boss(es) prepare their opening statement and what they want to achieve during the meeting. Coach them to request openness and to ensure no retribution when difficult topics are raised. Additionally, coach them to clearly state their expectation of the employees to focus on improving their working relationships.

Finally, discuss how you typically help during interactions within the group, and then ask if there are particular moments in which they would like your aid, such as listening during tense moments.

Interview the Employees: Talk to as many employees as possible and help determine what is working and not working and issues to be resolved. It is not always possible to interview employees. It is a best practice, yet not a showstopper.

Facilitator Preparation: Read the following: Chapters 7 and 8 of Volume I for basics in facilitation, the core triangle in tense moments, plus the concepts of neutrality and reciprocity; all chapters about SATA and Chapters 8 and 12 of *SOA*; and Appendix A, The SIPOC Model.

Length of Activity: This meeting lasts a full day. Length depends on the number of groups and people in attendance.

Room Setup: One flip chart and pens per breakout group. A large room is required with no tables, as participants will move around the room at different times.

Core Mental Models/Skills
- SATA (see *SOA*)
- SIPOC Model (Appendix A)
- Victim/Creator ("I" Language, Appendix B of Volume I)
- Behavior Description (Chapter 4 of *FFF*)
- Decision Making (Chapter 12 of *SOA*)
- Accountability (Chapter 7 of *SOA*)
- Follow-up (Chapter 10 of *SOA*)

Step-by-Step Agenda

1. Opening Statement
2. Introduce Facilitator
    *   Facilitator role
    *   Overview process
    *   Hand signal to manage group
3. Outcome Goals
    *   Managers present their goals
        o   Specific and measurable (if possible)
4. Generate Cross-Group Issues
    *   Present the SIPOC Model (see Appendix E)
    *   Break into separate workgroups
    *   Task Part 1
        o   Identify *major interfaces* using SIPOC Model
            ·   Identify *inputs.* Who supplies me with what?
            ·   Identify *outputs.* Who do I supply and with what?
    *   Task Part 2
        o   Generate issues around interfaces
            ·   For each interface, write on the flip chart what you want:
            ·   + *More of*
            ·   − *Less of*
            ·   = *Keep the Same*
    *   Choose a presenter for each group
5. Group Dialogue
    *   Explain dialogue rules
    *   Each group presents their entire list
    *   Capture issues and develop action plan (SPA, What, and By-When)
    *   Work Systemic Issues (SPA, SATA, Decision Clarity)
6. Close
    *   Set follow-up date

Agenda Explanation

Starting Room Setup: A large and dynamic activity requires space to allow participants to quickly move around the room. See Figure 1 for room setup.

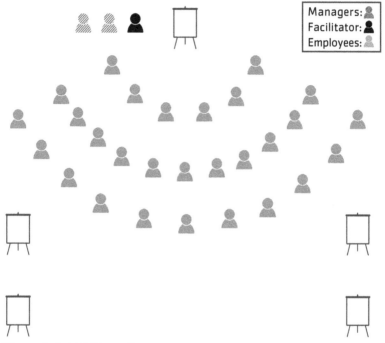

Figure 1 Initial Room Setup

Notice the flip charts (have one per group in the interaction) in the room from the beginning, which helps orient the participants to what will happen throughout the day.

Opening Statement: *The Initiating Sponsor (Single boss above all involved) or Sustaining Sponsors starts the meeting*, shares their hopes for the day, addresses meeting protocols, and then introduces the facilitator.

- **Sponsorship Clarity**—*Strong Sponsorship is critical in any intact workgroup or cross-group activities.* The boss of each group is, by definition, the Sponsor of their employees. *They decide when to start, not the facilitator, which is a core moment of meeting ownership.* If a boss asks me, "Should we get started?" Especially if people are late, I always respond with my opinion and say, "This is your meeting, start when you are ready." The boss(es) begins by stating the importance and desired outcomes of the meeting. *The boss(es) owns the meeting, not the facilitator.* If you think either boss does not want the meeting, then consider cancelling it.

Meeting Protocols:

- Expectations of participants.
- Put away all electronics (cell phones and laptops).
- Emergency procedures (safe meeting location).

    Ask for openness about the current cross-group situation. The manager must be clear that there will be no retribution if difficult topics are discussed. That expectation can only be fully ensured by each manager's boss (their Sponsor), yet the facilitator can ensure the whole system remains connected. Openness is critical to an engagement culture. Setting the stage and building trust with one's manager is an important part of these activities. Difficult topics must be addressed appropriately and resolved if possible, which builds trust and creates greater openness.

Optional Introduction Method - I have done some sessions where the employees did not know each other despite having to support each other. I start those sessions with the following activity:

- Ask the employees to stand up and walk around the room.
    - Greet people you know.
    - Introduce yourself to those you don't know.
        - What do you do?
        - What outcomes do you hope to see today?

Introduce Facilitator: The facilitator provides pertinent information about their background and then meets the participants (if interviews were not possible). The facilitator sets expectations about how they will help in tense moments and in other moments will add structural, cognitive, or behavioral theories to ensure effective outcomes. I typically say, "Please speak for yourself, and if tension arises, I may slow things down by asking one of you to repeat what you think the other said." Setting expectations is important to ensure people understand the process and, if tension does arise, are ready to do something different when asked.

Because this session can have large amounts of people (20–40) working in different areas and looking in different directions, I manage the room by introducing a *hand signal* to get people's attention. I say, "When I raise my hand, please finish your statement, stop talking, and also raise your hand. When you see others raising their hand, do the same. This allows me to interrupt gently to get your attention without raising my voice and lets you complete your thought." Once established, the hand signal to get people's attention is very effective.

After discussing expectations and setting up the hand signal to manage the group, review the agenda and the *context of the day*. For example, in Volume I for my chapter about intact work team development, I state, "The purpose of today is to create an even more effective work team."

Cross-group Context of the Day - A key to managing cross-group conflict is to help the groups learn from each other. Therefore, I normally say something like, "This day is a day of *discovery, learning,* and *understanding.*"

Outcome Goals: All involved managers share their goals. It is possible that one manager above all presents the overall goals of the day. Clarity of sponsorship is key, especially if there is high contention.

Additional Factors:

- **Fear of retribution**—Prepare the manager(s) if fear of retribution is present. The manager must acknowledge the fear and ensure there will be no retribution. You must contract with the boss for you to speak up immediately if their behavior appears as retribution. The objective is to slowly nurture employees to give and receive freely with no fear of (and no real) retribution. That takes time and sponsorship.

- **Focus on working relationships**—Prepare the managers to state, "you do not have to like each other but you do have to work together. You must provide cross-group needs such as the right information, materials, tools, and so on, with high quality and on time (as defined by when the other group needs it)."

Facilitator task during cross-group goals: *Opening Dialogue*—After the manager's opening statements and before the employees respond, have the employees *turn and talk* to the person beside them about the following:

- What do you like about the goals?
- What do you think you disagree with?
- What else do you want to learn?

Why *turn and talk* rather than simply starting the conversation with the total group? An engagement culture engages all employees. If you do not provide structured dialogue, then you will likely only hear from the extroverts. This small act breaks the typical patterns in the organization and gives everyone a voice. Plus, this actively engages all participants with content within 20 minutes of the meeting starting.

This *turn and talk* is a long-standing pattern breaker. Most have learned in school and at meetings that they can sit passively and not engage. Your task is to break that pattern and gently push the culture to interact. *The wording of the three questions is intentional.* Question two, for instance, is worded like this: "What do you think you disagree with?" It's important for people to understand that many disagreements come from misunderstandings. This wording gives employees license to raise disagreements without believing they know they disagree with the manager. That said, another option is asking, "What are you concerned or confused about?"

After the employees have talked to each other for a few minutes, open up the discussion to the total group. Then, help gain as much clarity of goals as possibly.

Generate Cross-Group Issues - At this stage the individual groups develop a list of items they want from the other groups.

Here is the progression to raise the issues for cross-group work.

1. **Present** the SIPOC Model (see Appendix A).
2. **Arrange the room** for the working session. Organize the participants by their function or workgroup. Figure 2 illustrates the room arrangement. Most rooms are not perfect squares. Do your best with the actual space to create functional, working arrangements.

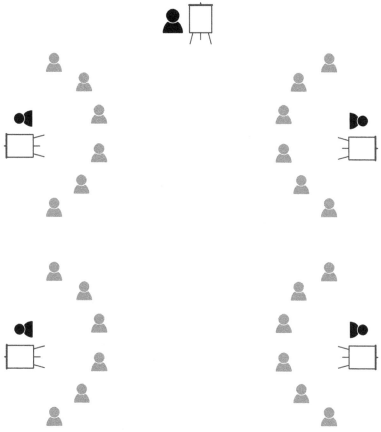

Figure 2 Group-by-Group Room Setup

- Generate cross-group issues.
  ○ Make a list of your internal customers and suppliers.
  ○ Identify what you want (+) *more of,* (−) *less of,* and (=) *keep the same* from each workgroup to achieve the goals. To illustrate, create a flip chart like Figure 14 on p.43.
- Check on the groups after 20–30 minutes. The length of time varies as employees work in groups and discuss what they want more of, less of, and same as. The output is to ensure the right issues are raised using constructive language.
- Make sure each group understands the instructions.
- Remind each group to select a presenter to share the data.
- Tell each group to add at least one praise (things they like and want to stay the same) for each department or group.

3. Sharpen the lists

- Review each list after 20–30 minutes. Figure 3 illustrates a flip chart created by a group that supports operations.

From Operations

+ Materials requested on time
+ Closing of orders and adjustments (includes bulk)
+ Deliver samples on time
+ Communication in case of aborted orders or problems online
+ Close communication with team leads and warehouse
+ Protection in change-over times

Figure 3 Cross-Group Feedback Example

Help the participants *change any interpretive word into a behavioral specific*. In this example I asked them to get specific by saying, "What does on time mean? Is there a service standard known, like within 30 minutes? Same question for how fast to close orders. What do you want communicated better with the warehouse and team leads? What do you consider protection?"

Then I often say, "You cannot solve general words like communication. You must articulate what they said or did or illustrate your exact meaning to create an effective plan to solve the problems." Behavioral specifics may require too many words for some items. In those cases, ensure the chart has no inflammatory words and the groups are ready with specific examples to illustrate the problem. This technique is similar to Chapters 3 and 4 of Volume I, except the participants write each topic on a flip chart. *The visual helps the facilitator notice words that are not behaviorally specific.* Figure 3 is one of five flip charts created by a group interacting with five groups that support a manufacturing floor.

Group Dialogue: Start the group dialogue using the following steps and processes.

- Start with the first group by having all participants arrange themselves where that group created their list (see Figure 4).

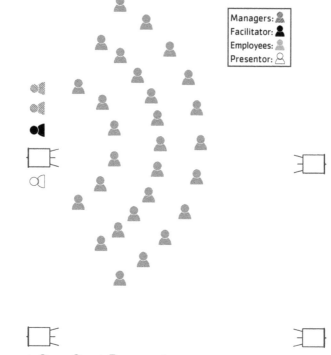

Figure 4 Cross-Group Presentations

- Meeting Rules for Cross-Group Dialogue
  - Presenter's job: Report what is on the list using nonblaming language.
  - Participants outside of presenting group: ask questions for clarity, meaning, and understanding.
  - Dialogue on each topic with the other members in the group filling in gaps from their position or experience related to the topic.
- Chart actions complete with SPA, What, By-When, and if others want to help on certain tasks, add a "work with" column to the action list.

After all issues are worked in the first group, it is the second group's turn to present their topics. Continue until all groups have presented. The facilitator brings the flip chart with the committed actions and expectations to each group and continues charting each new action or behavioral commitment during the entire session. Arrange participants around each area like they were for the first group.

During the dialogue your task is to help the group interact as constructively as possible by focusing on the following.

- Help the conversation go from general to specific. Meaning, notice discussions that start or remain at the judgment or interpretive level and help guide the conversation to specifics. Do so by asking for illustrations, specifics, or what the other said or did. For each general statement, the speaker normally has a specific example in mind. Do not allow the group to waste time arguing judgments or generalities.
- State decision clarity. The conversation is, at its heart, a consultative process between the boss(es) and employees. Meaning, the employees have influence, yet the boss(es) has the final decision.
- Track actions and behavioral expectations using task component clarity (see Figures 5 and 6).

Who (SPA)	What	By When
Joe	Create training matrix complete with who, what, and by-when. With input from group, review during one-on-one's.	6/24/2017
Jane	Create form to track issues and a visual board to track % complete of machine builds.	6/15/2017
Mary	Check new database status and report during next team meeting.	6/1/2017
Tom	Talk to inside sales about new plant startup and project specifics.	6/1/2017

Figure 5 In Dialogue Tracking—Action List

- Encourage participants to speak for self ("I" language).
- When tension rises, use the John Wallen *skills* to help people connect and slow down the conversation.
- If employees are talking about people in the room, then help them talk directly to the person. The mental model is called *triangulation.*
- If the boss struggles to create an action that is clear, then provide assistance by stating what you think is the action.

- If the boss is assigning themselves most of the actions, then help them delegate actions appropriately.
- If an employee is nervous to mention something that you think may not necessarily be a big issue, then support the employee to raise it and have a constructive dialogue.
- Notice employees politely waiting for their turn that others do not notice and call on them (gate keeping).
- Help the boss slow down if creating actions too fast before learning enough from the group.
- At the end of the dialogue, ask if you can do all this given your current resources? If not, what actions shall be delayed?

Behavioral Expectations

All	If other departments in the organization come to you with work or projects, take it but copy me on email.
All	If you are traveling, I want you to call and say if you need to stay, or if you are done. I will let you do what you think is right barring contractual obligations. If Tom is gone, then leave a voicemail. If you know that Tom won't be in (i.e., he is on vacation), then call Frank and Tom's boss to let them know.
All	If you have an issue with another person, then you need to tell them directly using behaviorally specific, nonblaming language.
All	If you are removed from working on a machine, then you must inform the appropriate team members.
Tom	I will create one-on-one meetings with each of you. Starting in July, I will meet with each of you one time per month.

Figure 6 In Dialogue Tracking - Behavioral Expectations

Given this is a cross-group process, knowledge of the SATA map is critical to help the group function properly. Therefore:

- If a boss is not engaging in a conversation about an issue that involves their workgroup, and their sponsorship is needed to solve it or let it go, then ask the boss to engage.
- Help bosses over all employees break ties as needed.

Work through Systemic Issues: A systemic issue is when I think my boss expects something that is different from what your boss expects. Mostly it happens unintentionally and always can be remedied by clarity and sponsorship.

Clarity means clear roles, boundaries, decision making, priorities, goals, and so on. These areas are systemic in nature and can be raised and heightened. During cross-group sessions, I often create a flip chart of expectations where, through dialogue, we chart who does what at certain times. For cross-group decision clarity, I use a simple grid (see p. 86) to ensure clarity of who decides and who gives input.

A good consultant/facilitator also listens for deeper role clarity issues that must be solved; extra sessions can be scheduled to resolve those problems. Two things are important when working role clarity. First, clarifying your role. Second, implementing a strategy to minimize requests outside of your job duties from the rest of the organization.

Once *clarity through dialogue is obtained*, then the Sustaining Sponsors must hold the people accountable to the new commitments. Generative power is key, including sufficient follow-up until the work happens smoothly without glitches.

Close: After the issues in all groups are discussed, use the following process to rate the session.

1. Make small pieces of paper or use 1 1/2 inch Post-it notes.

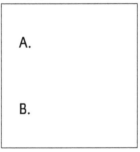

Figure 7 Example Small Survey

2. Use a flip chart to duplicate Figure 8.
3. Distribute a small piece of paper to each participant.
4. Tell them to:
    a. Write down letter *A* and *B* as shown.
    b. Do not include your name.
    c. The purpose is to receive semi-anonymous feedback.
5. Ask the following questions:
    A. What is your confidence level that we raised the right issues?

    B. What is your confidence level that we created the right

       actions and behavioral expectations to address the issues?

    Rate each on a scale of 1–10, with 10 being high.

6. When completed, fold your survey and pass it around the room.
At some point say, "OK, now all of you need to have a survey, and
if you get your own, just don't tell anyone." Occasionally somebody will say, "Oh I got my own," but it really doesn't matter.

7. By a show of hands, write the number on the flip chart corresponding to each score. This immediately rates the session.

Confidence level that we:

Raised the right Issues

Lo   Hi

1   2   3   4   5   6   7   8   9 10

A. ⬚⬚⬚⬚⬚⬚⬚⬚⬚⬚

Created the right Actions

Lo   Hi

1   2   3   4   5   6   7   8   9 10

B. ⬚⬚⬚⬚⬚⬚⬚⬚⬚⬚

Figure 8 Closing Survey Scoring Sheet

    Ask the group if anyone would like to say any closing words. Offer the
manager(s) to have the final comments. The meeting is now finished. *The
closing process* of rating the meeting can be used to *rate any session quickly*
and is a nice way to get all the opinions visible immediately. The process
also serves as a gut check for those who often complain after the session.
It is harder to take one negative voice seriously if most rated a session an
8 or higher. In the unlikely event that the scores are low, it provides an
opportunity to ask the group what issues or actions were missed.

    Additionally, ensure that the manager(s) schedule and share a follow-
up date. That date should be dependent on the following:

- How much pain is there in the workgroup?
- What dates are on the action list?

A typical time frame is about 6 weeks, but that could be adjusted
based on the various factors.

Follow-Up Process: This process takes about two hours. Once the meeting starts, I normally say something like,

"OK, I have a simple process to go through to work these issues. A major step in follow-up is simply having them. So give yourself credit for just being here. Now, I want you to rate the actions and commitments from the work team meeting on two dimensions."

Use the following process to rate the issues and expectations and generate constructive conversation.

1. **Step One:** Pass out commitments.
   - Hand each person a copy of the commitments and actions.
   - Have them number each commitment and action.
   - Have them draw a line on the right-hand side of the list creating two columns (see Figure 9).
2. **Step Two:** Rate commitments.
   - Rate each action or expectation on the following dimensions:
     - Are they done?
     - Are you getting the intended results?
   - Rate both dimensions on a scale of 1–10, with 10 being high.

#	Who (SPA)	What	By When	(1–10) Done	(1–10) Results
1	Joe	Create training matrix complete with who, what, and by-when. With input from group, review during one-on-one's.	6/24/2017	5	3
2	Jane	Create form to track issues and a visual board to track % complete of machine builds.	6/15/2017	7	5
3	Mary	Check new database status and report during next team meeting.	6/1/2017	1	1
4	Tom	Talk to inside sales about new plant startup and project specifics.	6/1/2017	8	6

Behavioral Expectations

#	Who	What	Done	Results
5	All	If other departments in the organization come to you with work or projects, take it but copy me on email.	8	9
6	All	If you are traveling, I want you to call and say if you need to stay, or if you are done. I will let you do what you think is right barring contractual obligations. If Tom is gone, then leave a voicemail. If you know that Tom won't be in (i.e., he is on vacation), then call Frank and Tom's boss to let them know.	6	6
7	All	If you have an issue with another person, then you need to tell them directly using behaviorally specific, nonblaming language.	4	9
8	All	If you are removed from working on a machine, then you must inform the appropriate team members.	9	10
9	Tom	I will create one-on-one meetings with each of you. Starting in July, I will meet with each of you one time per month.	10	7

Figure 9 Follow-up Example

While participants are rating, they often say, "How can I rate this. I do not know anything about it?" If so, I add extra rules such as, "OK, if you do not know but you need to, then write a zero. And, if you do not know and do not need to, then you can leave it blank. However, I prefer you stretch yourself and give your opinion on each one."

3. **Step Three:** Gather the data.

- Go one question at a time around the group.
- The first person reports their score and you capture it on the flip chart; then go to the second person and continue until you have captured all scores for Action 1.
- Only allow participants to report the numbers.
- Move to Action 2 and repeat the process.
- Be disciplined and do not allow explaining during this step. Tell the group that dialogue is the next step.

This method only takes a few minutes to gather the data. Stick with the rules by gently reminding them that each item will be discussed during the next step. Figure 10 illustrates an example of the final numbers.

Item #	(1-10) Done					(1-10) Results				
1.	8	1	8	7	5	3	5	1	6	3
2.	6	1	8	7	7	3	5	1	3	5
3.	7	1	1	3	1	3	1	1	5	1
4.	9	1	1	8	8	3	5	1	6	6
5.	9	0	8	10	8	3	0	9	7	9
6.	6	1	8	7	6	3	5	1	6	6
7.	6	1	8	7	4	3	5	1	6	9
8.	6	1	8	7	9	3	5	1	6	10
9.	10	9	10	1	10	7	6	10	1	7

Figure 10 Follow-up Compiled Ratings of All Employees

This engagement tool helps employees increase openness (Vol I, p. xx) about what is working and not working. It gives equal airtime to all employees and a quick visual rating of each commitment. The next step is to have a dialogue to understand what is underneath the ratings. Apply the following rules for the dialogue.

- If many actions, then apply the rule *ask* or *tell*.
  - Go to the action that you want to learn, and *ask* a question.
  - Go to the action that you want others to learn about and *tell* them what you want them to know.
- If a small amount of actions, then address each item.
- Hear explanations from the SPA who worked on the action.
- Learn from others about the action.
- Talk about what is working and not working.
- Generate or adjust actions as needed.
- Review the section on page 22, *during the dialogue*.

Effective follow-up is a dialogue intended to continue momentum toward lasting solutions. Many solutions need small tweaks, and some actions may need to be added or deleted. Formal follow-up allows for reflection, decisions on actions, and engagement from employees to ensure the right course is taken to achieve the goals.

If you have more than 20 people, then forgo rating each item and break into small groups to work specific issues, discuss what is working or not working, add additional actions or make small tweaks, and then report individual group findings to the whole group as part of a closing process. See page 98 for an example planning session follow-up and adapt it to your situation.

Success Variables

In Chapter 4, Workgroup Development of Volume I, I wrote the following:

"The two biggest success factors of this event are how well is it *sponsored* and effectively *followed up*.

Sponsorship is multidimensional. If the session is self-generated and condoned by the boss, then sponsorship, by definition, is in. If the manager's boss mandates the session, then that boss must clarify the importance to the manager. If the manager does not want the activity, but the boss says it must be done to solve specific items, then the event can still be successful.

A common mistake is to think improvement only happens if the person wants it. Strong sponsorship from the right person means *the manager does not have to like it but is willing to do it.* Leaders must use *generative power* to ensure growth is not optional in organizations, yet many avoid such conflicts (*SOA*, p. 71).

The second factor is follow-up, which requires formal and informal follow-up. Each leader must work the action list from the beginning and use 'The Fundamentals of Follow-up Check List' to ensure effective, informal follow-up (*SOA*, p. 149). At least one formal follow-up should happen as explained on the previous pages."

The same holds true here plus the *complexity that happens when there are multiple Sustaining Sponsors.* Best practice is for the boss (Initiating Sponsor), directly above all other bosses, to understand, own, and drive the follow-up. Depending on the complexity, follow-up could mean checking in from time to time or holding weekly cross-group meetings with key participants for a more structured approach. The Initiating Sponsor must remain aware of the progress and intervene as needed. If things are working well, then no different behavior is required.

Optional Add-ons

This activity can be adapted to meet whatever needs you are trying to achieve by additional developmental theories. My favorite add-ons are from Volume I, Appendix A, SOCIAL STYLE⁻ and Appendix B, Victim/Creator.

SOCIAL STYLE explains internal tension and blind spots that may or may not be happening in the group. It is perfect for intact workgroups. The most striking example was when a group was talking about one machine creating half of the scrape in the plant and costing millions per month. One participant suggested to study the machine for the next several months to understand the issues, yet many in the group already articulated specific pain caused by the machine. I then stated, "According to the SOCIAL STYLE chart on this lead team, you will talk about this for months, maybe years and not make a decision." (See an example SOCIAL

STYLE systemic chart on p. 120 of Volume I.) The SOCIAL STYLE chart placed almost all of the lead team members in either the Analytical Style or Amiable Style quadrant and none in the Driving Style quadrant. At that point the plant manager said something like, "Wow, OK I am going to put in an RFA tomorrow to replace the machine."

Victim/Creator is profound in its ability to focus on self-improvement versus blaming other groups. "Fix our house first before complaining about the neighbors," as one client told his direct reports. This does not exclude raising issues that are truly about working better with other groups as remedies to input or output needs.

Additionally, cross-group work benefits greatly from John Wallen's *The Interpersonal Gap* (Chapter 3 of *FFF*), which adds a frame for how to manage tense moments.

Any add-ons go between Steps 2 and 3 of the agenda because they frame the day and give mental models to use during tense moments that may arise. Call it "group development" or use the theory name. I normally name Victim/Creator, "culture of accountability" because I have them focus on core items regarding accountability in the context of the conversation.

Integration with Chapter 4

Use the system-wide process improvement outlined in Chapter 4 and the cross-group activity in this chapter to flush and address all issues. Informal processes exist within organizations that have continued to evolve with less than stellar consequences. Meaning, a solution was applied to a problem without addressing the root cause; thus, the process became dysfunctional. Therefore, the organization tries to manage their cross-functional process through signoffs and extra steps.

Instead, improve the process and manage the employees. If someone is abusing a process, then help the sponsor manage the individual. I worked with an inside sales group in a manufacturing plant and an off-site warehouse that had processes out of control. We started with the system-wide process improvement activity to align and learn each step of the process (see Chapter 4). We followed up with several cross-group meetings, discussing what was working and not working. During later sessions we fine-tuned the process until it was running smoothly.

Breaking Silos: Part 1

I define a silo *as any two departments that need to give and receive product, information, tools, services, and other items to and from each other who are struggling to do so and/or potentially behaving in ways that Gallup calls actively disengaged.* This chapter is Part 1 of the four step-by-step guides to break silos and improve how groups work together to achieve daily tasks. Chapters 3, 4, and 5 provide guides to solve other core areas involved in breaking silos.

Breaking silos at work is a difficult yet worthy objective that *can* and *should* be accomplished. Beyond any process, **the key to breaking silos is strong sponsorship** using generative power (see *SOA*).

Multiple strategies, time, and energy are required to be successful and consistent application of generative power. You cannot break a silo nor manage any emotional issue from afar. Therefore, to succeed in resolving workplace silos, you must make sure you have the *time* and *energy* to endure until the groups are consistently working well together. In some ways that is the simple definition of effective ***Sponsorship—the ability to stay firm and stick to a problem until it is completely solved.***

Conclusion

The group-to-group conflict process is a simple and effective way to improve the connection between groups. It is not only for conflict moments. The process can and should be used periodically to ensure that interconnected groups provide each other the right materials, supplies, products, and services with quality and on time.

CHAPTER 3

Goal Alignment

All workplaces are trying to achieve goals. This engagement strategy centers around those goals. The process creates or sharpens your organization's measurable goals, aligns your employees, ensures they understand their purpose and priorities, and sets in motion a plan for achievement. In contrast, misaligned workplaces often waste time blaming people, groups, or processes for their failure to achieve results.

Introduction

What follows is an extension of Chapter 2, Goals of *SOA*, which outlines a process called goal alignment. This chapter provides step-by-step instructions for that process.

The process involves working with the lead team of the plant and then cascading a similar group process throughout the organization. The result is that *all employees* will accomplish the following:

- Reach goal clarity.
- Raise issues to achieve the goals.
- Influence which issues to solve.
- Develop actions to solve selected issues.
- Implement those actions.
- Follow up until issues are resolved and goals are obtained.

This process builds sponsorship throughout the organization because each manager sharpens their goals and better understands what is expected of them, shares them with their employees, and, through an interactive process, sets in motion a plan for achievement.

To align an organization, the top leader must sharpen the goals to be as measurable and clear as possible, then align their direct reports to those goals. Start with a dialogue on the overall goals followed by each report developing department goals to fit the overall goals. Include feedback across departments on inputs required from each department to accomplish the goals.

Why? When managers are highly aligned to each department's goals and the inputs that are needed from the other departments to succeed, then the amount of competing priorities and confusion throughout the organization decreases exponentially. Misalignment is often manifested in blame of one department or another.

An aligned organization requires dialogue, focus, precision, and persistence, followed by diligent conversations to maintain alignment. Please do not expect to align a complex organization by handing goals to each department and hoping that they do the right thing. All workgroups are in some state of alignment: between highly aligned to very much out of alignment.

Dialogue is required to build and maintain alignment. Calm leaders understand and remain persistent during moments of misalignment when slight shifts are required. The question is not if you will get out of alignment but, rather, when. Then, how quickly is it recognized, and will you be ready with a response that calms the organization? Or will you hurt alignment by giving a reactive response? My hope is that you will return the organization to alignment with calm and consistent leadership.

Prepare for Lead Team Session

Prepare for goal alignment by sharpening the initiating or location leaders' goals. In some cases the location has matrixes and dotted and solid line reporting relationships. Yet, in all cases the bottom-line goals (BLG) for that location must be achieved for success within the existing reporting structure.

Goal alignment in a *highly matrixed* world is critical because, by definition, if there are *more bosses*, then there are *more opportunities for unintended competing priorities*. No matter what your structure, an effective process of goal alignment will likely uncover competing priorities. In the case of dotted and solid-line reporting relationships, by intentional use of SATA, you can set or confirm simple strategies to clear up priorities (see Figure 11).

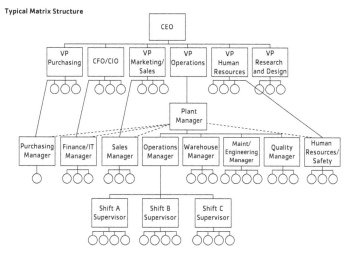

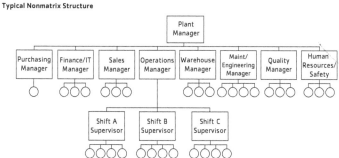

Figure 11 Matrix vs. Nonmatrix Goal Alignment

All structures have advantages and disadvantages. You must work within the organization's existing reality. Some situations, by simple math, create more opportunities for alignment issues. Matrix organizations allow for more technical expertise to directly lead departments, rather than relying on one boss understanding multiple disciplines. However, matrix organizations also complicate matters when quick decisions are needed on direction. Regardless of structure, simple strategies must be implemented to resolve competing priorities and moments of misalignment.

A structured group-by-group process to align goals allows employees, who are usually the first to experience the consequences of misalignment issues, to raise and resolve moments of confusion. As long as the leaders listen, which is part of effective facilitation, they can learn how to more effectively manage those moments.

Prepare the Boss: Task one is to sharpen the goals if needed. Learn about the organization's goals and coach the location leader to get them measurable and precise (see *SOA* Chapter 2, Goals and Appendix D). The focus is on BLGs for the location. Key initiatives, major projects, or broken processes may also require alignment at the lead team level. The core bottom line of the business must be worked at this level.

Interview the Employees: Interviewing and preparing the Initiating Sponsor is mandatory, while the remaining department heads is a "nice to have." If you can talk to department heads, then help them sharpen their department goals. Additionally, have them think about what is working and not working, and what issues must be resolved to achieve the goals.

If you are internal, you can develop clever ways to do this process over time and reduce the time needed with all participants together.

Facilitator Preparation: Read the following: Chapters 7 and 8 in Volume I for the core triangle in tense moments, plus the concepts of neutrality and reciprocity; Chapter 2 of *SOA*; and Appendix A, The SIPOC Model.

Length of Activity: The lead team meeting might take 2 days. The length of meeting depends on the number of add-ons and amount of attendees. The intact workgroup meetings (each group below the lead team) take 4–8 hours depending on group size. Manufacturing organizations with large shifts must adjust the meetings to be successful.

Goal alignment is intended to be cascaded to each workgroup. Doing the work at the lead team level is essential, but work with each intact workgroup to move a whole organization rapidly toward achieving goals.

Lead Team Room Setup: One flip chart and pens per department head or direct report in attendance. Use the same or similar setup as on page 15 of Chapter 2. Arranging tables in a U-shape would also be acceptable.

Intact Group Room Setup: One flip chart and pens. Arrange participants to ensure eye contact, as facial expressions help create dialogue. Advanced technology may alter your approach to capturing actions and behavioral expectations. Ensure the actions, theories, and commitments are easily visible to all participants as aids to understanding and dialogue.

Core Mental Models/Skills
- Rainbow Model of Goals (see p. 41 or p. 23 of *SOA*)
- The SIPOC Model (Appendix A)
- Victim/Creator ("I" Language, Appendix B of Volume I)
- Behavior Description (Chapter 4 of *FFF*)
- SATA (see *SOA*)
- Decision Making (Chapter 12 of *SOA*)
- Accountability (Chapter 7 of *SOA*)
- Follow-up (Chapter 10 of *SOA*)

Step-by-Step Agenda
(Lead Team)

1. Opening Statement
2. Introduce Facilitator
   - Facilitator role
   - Hand signal to manage group
3. Organization-Wide Goals
   - Dialogue
4. Develop Department Goals and Cross-Department Feedback
   - Present Rainbow Model of goals (see *SOA*, p. 23)
   - Present the SIPOC Model (see Appendix A)
   - Each department head creates their goals to reach the plant goals
   - Each department generates feedback to the other departments
     - What do they need
       - + *More* of
       - - *Less of*
       - = Keep the same
     - From the other departments to reach their goals
5. Group Dialogue
   - Department by department
     - Presents goals
     - Presents feedback
   - Develop actions to address feedback
   - Work systemic issues (SPA, SATA, Decision Clarity)
6. Close

Agenda Explanation

Opening Statement: The boss of the lead team starts the meeting by stating the day's purpose and their hopes for the location.

- Review the opening statement of Chapter 2 (or Chapters 3 and 4 of Volume I) and *incorporate as needed for your unique situation.*

Introduce Facilitator: See page 16 in Chapter 2. Include a brief explanation of the goal alignment process beyond the session with the lead team.

Organization-Wide Goals: The boss shares critical data that includes, but is not limited to:

- Current state of the marketplace.
- This location's position in the market.
- Likely outcomes and impacts of success and failures.
- *Measurable business goals* to improve market position.
- Major location-wide projects or initiatives to achieve success.
- Broken internal work processes that must be improved.

The location manager may need help clarifying these items from Sales, Finance, or other departments. This list is the minimum needed to help your employees understand the current state and why it is critical to improve.

Facilitator task during organizational-wide goals: *Opening Dialogue*—Same process as Chapter 2, except adjust your questions slightly to:

- What are you learning about the current state of the marketplace? Do you have anything to add?
- What do you like about the goals?
- What are you concerned or confused about?
- What else do you want to learn to understand the goals?

Develop Department Goals and Cross-Department Feedback: Each department manager or direct report of the location manager creates two items. First, the department goals that must be achieved to reach the overall plant goals. Second, cross-department feedback of what they need more of and less of from the other departments to reach those goals.

Regarding cross-department feedback, let's return to Gallup.

> "Gallup developed *State of the American Workplace* using data collected from more than 195,600 U.S. employees via the Gallup Panel and Gallup Daily tracking in 2015 and 2016, and more than 31 million respondents through Gallup's Q12 Client Database." (2017 *Gallup State of the American Workplace Report*)

Gallup's Q12 database contains 12 questions to track workplace engagement. The data found that "those companies that have the highest percentage of engaged employees have the best performance metric across the board." The first two survey questions address the basic needs of the employees. Question one is, "I know what is expected of me at work." Question two is, "I have the materials and equipment I need to do my work right." Both questions scored low, yet mirror my experience in organizations.

Clarity of goals directly relates to expectations, and cross-group feedback is critical to impact question two. In fact, regarding question two Gallup found that only "3 in 10 U.S. employees strongly agree they have the materials and equipment they need to do their work right." Further they state:

> ". . . by moving that ratio to six in 10 employees, organizations could realize an 11% increase in profitability, a 32% reduction in safety incidents, and a 27% improvement in quality."

Imagine the bottom-line impact if you could increase the number to 8 in 10? Goal alignment goes directly after this and helps the lead team step up into their emotional intelligence (EQ). I teach EQ workshops inside businesses, and part of the skill development is to learn how to state your wants to others in a nonblaming way. This skill has shown to be among the hardest of all participants to master regardless of their level in the organization. The good news is it can be learned, sponsored, and mandated, as it is necessary to function in the fast-paced working world in which we live.

Goal alignment is critical to break this pattern as it helps build appropriate sponsorship and provide the right venue for managers to learn. Perhaps the most important place to build the competencies to consistently provide cross-group feedback to achieve world-class results is at the lead team level.

Here is the progression to prepare for goal alignment.

1. **Present the Rainbow Model of Goals** and then the SIPOC Model (see Appendix A). Here is what I say and draw on a flip chart to present the Rainbow Model.

Rainbow Model

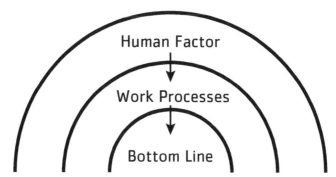

Figure 12 Rainbow Model of Goals

To present the Rainbow Model, I start with BLGs and say, "BLGs are the reason you exist. For example, for sales it could be total revenue; for production it could be product per day; for quality it could be amount of returns; and so on. Your job is to determine your BLGs unique to your location by your department. Because BLGs are the reason you exist (for sales, it is a specific revenue number). Work Process Goals (WPG) are how the work flows through each area. In other words, WPGs are your task inputs, throughputs, and outputs.

Finally, Human Factor Goals (HFG) are strategies to engage your employees. In other words, how will you engage your employees to improve the work processes that in turn will positively impact the bottom line." While I say the last sentence, I draw the arrows you see on Figure 12.

Then I draw a circle and say, "This circle represents a pie of the overall location goals. What is your piece of the pie?" See Figure 13.

Figure 13 *Goals as Pie Chart*

I then give a quick version of the SIPOC Model, as presented in Appendix A, where I emphasize internal customers and suppliers.

2. **Department Leads' Task.** After presenting the Rainbow Model of Goals, the SIPOC Model, and drawing the pie chart, I ask the leads to write the following on flip charts.

- **Department goals**
    ○ *1-2 BLGs*
    ○ *2-4* WPGs
    ○ *1-2* HFGs
- **Feedback to other departments**
    ○ Make a list of your internal customers and suppliers.
    ○ Identify what you want (+) *more of,* (−) *less of,* and (=) *keep the same* from each department to achieve your goals. For this part, I create a flip chart that looks like Figure 14.

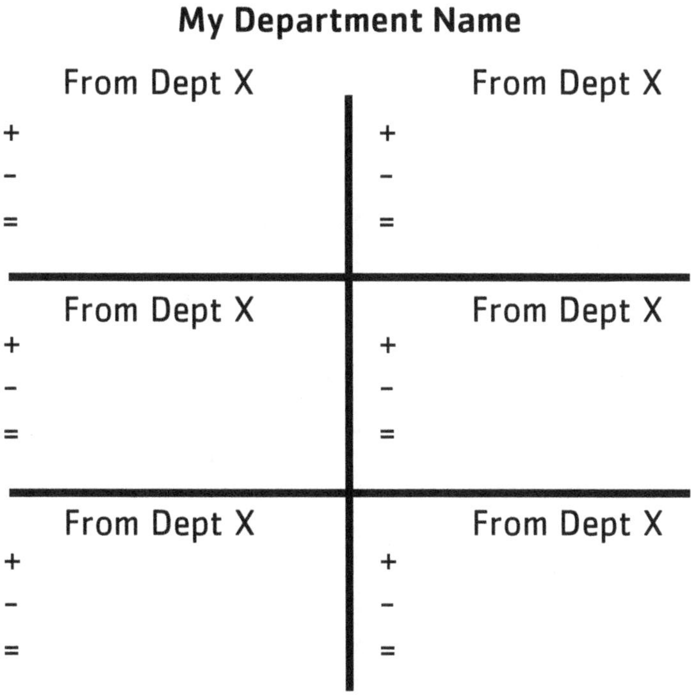

My Department Name

From Dept X	From Dept X
+ – =	+ – =
From Dept X	**From Dept X**
+ – =	+ – =
From Dept X	**From Dept X**
+ – =	+ – =

Figure 14 Blank Cross-Group Feedback Chart

- Be prepared to present your goals and feedback to all attendees.
- This exercise could last more than an hour. The outcome should be well thought-out goals and feedback. Unlike the larger cross-group process in Chapter 2, these groups are often small enough that people will work elsewhere to focus and ensure the exercise objectives are achieved. I just need to know where their location is, so I can effectively complete step three.

3. **Translate to Behavioral Specifics**
   - Work the lists that are created similar to other processes. Figure 15 shows an example more of chart before it was translated into behavioral specifics.

Production

Quality	Planning
+ Clear guidelines for out-of-spec product	+ Reduce amount of schedule changes
Warehouse	Human Resources
+ Material delivered on time	+ Fully staffed shifts
Maintenance	Sales
+ Full schedule for all machines	+ Accurate orders
Finance	Purchasing
+ Accurate numbers	+ Product in stock

Figure 15 Example of Partially Completed Feedback Chart

- Coach the participants to *change any interpretive words into behavioral specifics.* Chapter 2 (p.20) provides an example of how to translate words into behavioral specifics. Figure 15 needs help and contains potential clarifying questions in each category. The completed feedback charts should contain no interpretive words.
- Tell each group to add at least one praise (things they like and want to stay the same) for each department or group.

Group Dialogue: Start the group dialogue using the following steps and processes:

- Start with a department that is willing to go first.
- Ground rules for cross-group dialogue.
  - Presenters job—share the list using nonblaming language.
  - Participants outside of presenting group—ask questions for clarity, meaning, and understanding.
  - Dialogue on each topic with the other members in the group.

- Chart actions complete with SPA, What, By-When, and if others want to help on certain tasks, add a "work with" column to the action list.
- **Critical step at lead team level**—After each department head states their goals and has ensuing dialogue, turn to the location manager and ask, "Did they get it?" (i.e., "Are these the right goals for this department to reach the overall plant goals or did they miss something? If he missed something, what is it?") Repeat this process for each department.

During the dialogue use the guidelines in Chapter 2 (p. 22) plus:

- When working systemic issues, listen for moments when cross-group decision making is not clear and be ready with a decision matrix (see p. 148).

Close: See page 24 of Chapter 2 and close the same way, except ask the following questions.

 i. What is your confidence level that in this session we achieved *clarity of goals?*
 ii. What is your confidence level that in this session we raised the *right issues?*
 iii. What is your confidence level that in this session we generated the *right actions* to address the issues and reach the goals?
 iv. Rate each question on a scale of 1–10, with 10 being high.

If these ratings reveal that most think one or more categories is low, then have the group turn and talk in pairs about which issues are missing. Then work those issues and rescore.

Prepare for the next steps: Ensure the managers understand the process below the lead team level. Show them the agenda at that level (see p. 46), and explain how the sessions will differ from the lead team session.

Clarify the dates, including follow-up. A typical time frame for follow-up is about 6 weeks, but that could be adjusted based on various factors.

Follow-Up Process—See guidelines created in Chapter 2.

Step-by-Step Agenda
(Intact Workgroup)

1. Opening Sponsor Statement
2. Introduce Facilitator
   - Facilitator role
3. Department or Work Team Goals (Bottom Line, Work Process, Key Initiatives)
   - Dialogue
4. Issue Raising
   - Group raises issues that must be addressed to reach the goals
   - Dialogue on each issue
     - Develop actions to solve issues (SPA, What, By-When)
   - Work systemic issues (SPA, SATA, Decision Clarity)
5. Close
   - Set follow-up date

Agenda Explanation

Opening Statement: The Sustaining Sponsor, by definition the boss of the intact group, starts the meeting by stating the day's purpose and hopes for the work team.

- Review the opening statement sections of Chapters 2 and *incorporate as needed for your unique situation.*

Introduce Facilitator: See Chapter 2 (p.16). Explain the goal alignment process beyond just the session with the lead team.

Department or Work Team Goals: The boss shares what was learned about the current state that is relevant to the work team. That may include the following:

- Current state of the marketplace.
- This location's position in the market.
- Likely outcomes and impacts of success and failures.
- *Measurable business goals* to improve market position.
- Major location-wide projects or initiatives to achieve success.
- Broken internal work processes that must be improved.

I present a thumbnail on the Rainbow Model and then have the boss provide the goals. The manager presents their goals, as clarified with the lead team, in all three categories.

Facilitator task during workgroup goals: *Opening Dialogue*—Same process as Chapter 2, except adjust your questions slightly to:

- What are you learning about the current state of the marketplace? Do you have anything to add?
- What do you like about the goals?
- What are you concerned or confused about?
- What else do you want to learn about the goals to be ready to raise issues that must be solved to achieve them?

Issue Raising: The group develops a list of issues that must be solved to reach their goals. What follows is the same four-step process explained in Chapter 4 of Volume I, except here I do not use a survey. Instead, in step one, I prompt the group to think about common issues by saying something like, "You are about to raise issues that you think need to be addressed to reach the goals, including how you work together as a team or what you get from other departments. You may have times that the inputs you need do not arrive on time and with quality. You may need more authority to make quick decisions. You may need more help at times to make decisions. You may think your meetings are not working. You could be meeting too much or not enough."

My goal is to prompt opportunities and help them raise real situations. From here follow the same issue-raising guidelines from step two to four.

Use the following progression to raise issues and generate constructive conversation.

1. **Step One**
   - Prompt the group as stated above.
   - The boss can leave or stay. If the boss leaves, I instruct them to develop a list of issues to address upon returning.

2. **Step Two**
   - Work in pairs.
   - Develop two lists.
     - What issues must be addressed and solved to reach the goals?
     - What you want to *stay the same* or maintain (praises of the boss or group)
   - Reaffirm that the list is to solve problems and issues in the way of reaching the goals.
   - Give the group 20 minutes and assist as needed.
   - Affirm that any topic can be addressed.

3. **Step Three**
   - After a few minutes, remind each pair to list all items regardless if they are in agreement. The act of pairing is *not intended to be an act of creating consensus*, but rather to fully engage each group participant, build working relationships, and have a partner to help generate topics.

4. **Step Four**
   - After 20 minutes, check each group's list. Coach the participants to change any interpretive word into a behavioral specifics (see Chapter 4 of FFF). I sometimes allow them to illustrate their topic, but I do not want any harsh judgments, as it will create

a predictable argument unless it is being said to a savvy and highly emotionally intelligent boss.

○ This step is the key to the kingdom for constructive conversation and a real engagement culture. Work cultures that do not engage do so, at least in part, because they are unclear about the distinction between a judgment and a behavioral specific. Consequently, employees that have tried to have difficult conversations have typically led with a negative judgment. This approach creates tension and increases the odds of a poor outcome. Most bosses struggle to remain constructive when an employee raises a difficult topic by starting with a negative judgment of them.

Alternate data collection method: Once the pairs have finished their initial lists, capture the list as a group on the flip chart. Go pair by pair, with the facilitator writing one item on the flip chart at a time, per pair, then capturing the next item from the next pair. The facilitator continues around the room until all items are captured. If pairs have duplicates, they are marked off their list. This method allows the facilitator to ensure all items are addressed and uses the wording of items to help teach the group about behavioral specifics. Thus, the group learns that skill together. The downside is that it takes extra time before the manager returns and the dialogue starts.

When you use this method, you must also add a discussion about who presents the data to the manager. Here are your choices. 1) The person who raised it says it. This may seem like a logical choice, yet many have the same item on their list, and in some situations, raising this question helps the employees build their fear of too much openness. 2) Have a spokesperson start the conversation and then involve those who share the issue in the dialogue. The problem with Option 2 is that it lets employees pass on starting a dialogue by speaking directly to the boss. Only use this option as a last resort in moments of high tension. Tell the group the process is Option 1, and only add Option 2 if needed.

This chapter is continued with the data collection method, where each pair's list remains with them. I raised the alternate data collection method because it has merit. Use it when the situation benefits from extra control by the facilitator, such as when there is high tension between the boss and employees.

Group Dialogue: When the boss returns to the room, prepare for the dialogue by giving the following guidelines.

- Explain *reciprocity* and that you will track actions and behavioral expectations.
- Start with the first pair raising a topic. They can raise either an *issue* or a *same as* (praise).
- Share praises directly to the boss. There are three options: 1) Start by having each pair share a praise and continue until all praises are shared, 2) have each pair share one praise and then share an issue, 3) use Option 1, but at the end of the meeting. *Positive feedback is perhaps the most underused feedback in organizations.* Before the meeting ends, make sure the group shares their praise lists.
- After that issue is worked in the group, move to the next pair and continue around the circle until *all* items are worked. You will likely go around the circle multiple times.
- Each item raised is intended for a whole group dialogue.
- To start the dialogue, encourage *the employee* who wanted the issue/item on the list to *say it directly to the boss.*
  - *Beginning facilitators often fail at this moment.* The core concept is about who gives the data to whom. *This moment is key to develop an engagement culture because it teaches employees to be direct even if the issue is difficult or complicated.* Use these moments to help employees build the capacity to talk directly to their boss about issues no matter how apparently difficult. This increases trust and deepens the boss–employee relationship. Gallup confirms that the key to an engagement culture is strengthening the working relationship between boss and employee.

    Intact workgroup meetings may include difficult topics that employees have avoided raising to the boss for a variety of reasons. Using a trained facilitator presents a great opportunity to build confidence and strengthen the boss-employee relationship, which is the key to an engagement culture.

In an engagement culture all layers can talk directly to each other, and all issues can be worked directly. This is not to say it is a free-for-all. In fact, clearly aligned leadership is critical for an engagement culture. Yet, the core tenet is the ability to speak directly to each other in nonjudgmental and therefore behaviorally specific ways. Thus, this group will practice doing just that.

- The first task of the boss when their employee raises their issue is to listen and articulate their understanding of the item as behaviorally specific as possible. Then a constructive dialogue ensures each employee adds what they think, responds to each other, fills the gaps, and eventually the group works toward potential solutions.

Intact workgroup goal alignment meetings tend to create 8–15 actions and a list of behavioral expectations to improve the outputs of the team and solve their issues.

During the dialogue use the guidelines in Chapter 2 (p. 22) plus:
- When working systemic issues, listen for moments when cross-group decision making is not clear and be ready with a decision matrix (see p. 86).

Close: Apply the same process from Chapter 2 (p. 24), but ask the following questions.

   i. What is your confidence level that in this session we achieved *clarity of goals?*
   ii. What is your confidence level that in this session we raised the *right issues?*
   iii. What is your confidence level that in this session we have generated the *right actions* to address the issues and reach the goals?
   iv. Rate each question on a scale of 1–10, with 10 being high.

If these ratings reveal that most think one or more categories is low, then have the group turn and talk in pairs about which issues are missing. Then work those issues and rescore.

Finally, have the manager confirm the follow-up date.

Working with a Manufacturing Floor

Of course, not all groups operate the same. In fact, large groups, such as a manufacturing floor, need a different format and structure during the issue-raising portion to work through the issues. Use the following process with groups of 15 or more.

Step-by-Step Agenda
(Intact Workgroup of 15 or more)

1. Opening Sponsor Statement
2. Introduce Facilitator
    *   Facilitator role
3. Department or Work Team Goals (Bottom Line, Work Process, Key Initiatives)
    *   Dialogue
4. Issue Raising
    *   Group identifies four to five problems to address
    *   Create workgroups (four to five people per group)
    *   Brainstorm barriers to problem
    *   Whole group activity: share with all employees
    *   Develop actions to solve issues (SPA, What, By-When)
5. Close
    *   Set follow-up date

Agenda Explanation

Use the same room setup in Chapter 2 for this process. The agenda is the same for steps 1, 2, 3, and 5 as the last agenda. Therefore, I will only review step 4, the new process, and room setup.

Issue Raising—At this stage the group decides on the critical problems/issues to be solved to achieve the goals and breaks into small groups to work on one specific problem.

1. **Generate problems:** Have employees work in groups of three and discuss the most important problems to solve to reach the work team goals. This should take 5–10 minutes, and you may have to remind people that we are not solving the problem right now; we are just identifying the problems.

2. **Capture:** Capture one item per group from their list and then move to the next group. Repeat the process until all items are captured. Tell the groups that if their issue is already captured, then cross it off their list. If there is debate about duplication, then capture both and clarify later as needed. Do not allow one group to give their entire list at once, as that hurts the interactive flow of the room and allows introverts off the hook of voicing their issues.

3. **Multivote:** Count the issues (and number them while doing so) and tell people they each get 20% of the total number on which to vote. Give these instructions: "OK, you each get x amount of votes. You can raise your hand once per item, and you must use all your votes. Don't worry; the votes only provide information as to what you think is most important. They will not be the final say." A typical number of issues is around 20, which means they all get four votes.

4. **Select:** The group reviews the votes and chooses four to five problems. Combine items if they are similar and specify the meaning of the problem being advocated. Ensure you guide the process instead of making the decision. This process is a consultative process, with the manager having the final say. Obvious problems often arise which makes it easy to choose, yet sometimes the manager must step up to get the group focused on what they think are the right problems.

5. **Determine groups:** Place a flip chart with the selected problems in each corner or specific area of the room and have the employees go to the flip chart with the problem they want to resolve. Then, while still standing, adjust the groups by allowing people to advocate for other employees. The boss has the final say, and each group requires at least four people for effective brainstorming. If one group is much larger than others, they will take longer and disrupt the timing. Balance is required for the process to work.

Brainstorm: Have the groups brainstorm barriers to solving the problem following the process in Appendix E.

Whole group activity: Share the data by having the employees follow the same process in Chapter 5 (p. 81).

Develop actions: Have each group develop a list of actions (SPA, What, By-When) to overcome each barrier and solve the problem.

Some create actions easier than others. Observe the process and help the right people get involved at the right times. Often it takes the manager driving this stage; yet other times the actions can come from the group. The best process is another full round of brainstorming to develop the actions as described in Chapter 5, which takes another few hours. *The trap to avoid is leaving a meeting with no actions. That creates panic and loss of direction.* Managers sometimes appoint people to develop actions and schedule a meeting to share the actions. This approach can also work, though it may reduce ownership because the group is less involved in the process and, therefore, it could be less effective.

Close: Announce the follow-up date and close the same way as the previous sessions. Use the same process as on page 45. You may only ask questions ii and iii if you wish.

Cascade Process

Goal alignment is intended to be cascaded to every workgroup. I highly recommend doing the whole process once each year. However, you can also use any process in this chapter as a standalone.

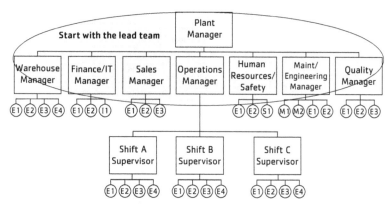

Figure 16 Cascade Goal Alignment Example-Lead Team

To cascade the process, *start with the lead team* and apply the process and agenda from the beginning of this chapter (see p. 38).

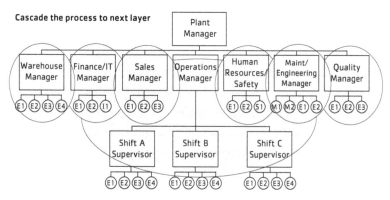

Figure 17 Cascade Goal Alignment-Department Leads

Then move to the next level down from the lead team (see Figure 17). This level is the department heads who report to the location leader and their direct reports (see agenda on p. 46).

If the organization is matrixed, then the process still involves anyone who leads a department, even if their solid line reporting relationship is to corporate. Help the location leader build sponsorship to ensure all matrixed leaders participate.

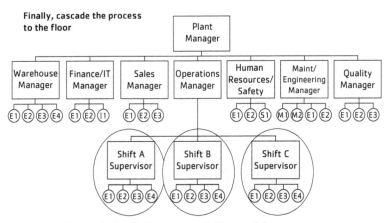

Figure 18 Cascade Goal Alignment-Additional Layers

Continue the process through each layer until all workgroups have participated. If the workgroup is large (more than 15 people), then choose a different format to manage the group (see p. 52).

KRID

System-wide, workgroup goal alignment (along with Chapter 4 in Volume I) is perhaps the biggest bang for your buck in terms of rapid culture change toward increased results and improved morale. Cascade the process to each workgroup and then help the organization manage the issues that arise by building sponsorship at the right levels and using a variation of the process called KRID.

KRID stands for Knowledge Retrieval Implication Derivation (see Appendix B). Apply the following KRID after all workgroups complete their sessions. Prepare a large room and have all managers and other key people join the closing process (end of initial work sessions).

1. **Step One:** Whole group reviews work session outputs
   - Review list of session ratings (See closing ratings. The facilitator must save each one.)
   - Review master list of SOCIAL STYLE (Take pictures and put dots on the SOCIAL STYLE grid color coded by work team.)
   - Review total list of actions (by having the actual flip charts of lists or an Excel of all actions per group) and ask, "Do we have too many actions based on our resources? Are there duplicate

actions and if so, are they necessary? If unnecessary, which person in what group should take the action?"

2. **Step Two:** Share in small groups
   - Talk to each other in small groups (three to four) to discuss learnings, share issues, and clarify actions raised in each session. After 5 to 10 minutes, switch groups and repeat. Continue until all participants have interacted, if possible.

3. **Step Three:** Derive implications
   - Pair and derive implications to the organization.
   - Suggest actions and decide in a consultative conversation with the Initiating Sponsor in the room.

Combine this with other activities in the both volumes to improve multiple places in an organization in short manner. Of course, the activities in these books are not the only way to achieve an engaged culture. Use them with other methods you may have learned, such as Lean, Six Sigma, or other problem-solving means. Once the organization is aligned as defined in my first book, *Strategic Organizational Alignment*, then all problem-solving methods become more effective.

Optional Add-ons

This activity can be adapted to meet whatever needs you are trying to achieve by adding developmental theories. My favorites are Appendix A, SOCIAL STYLE and Appendix B, Victim/Creator both of Volume I. I almost always use SOCIAL STYLE and Victim/Creator when working with lead teams. When cascading a process for the first time, I normally use the Victim/Creator in each group. Any add-ons go between Steps 2 and 3 of the agenda because they frame the day and give mental models to use during tense moments that may arise.

Breaking Silos: Part 2

Measurable goals are key to breaking silos. Why? Without measurable goals, employees only work toward *what they think* is the right direction. When employees know how they are measured and how it fits into the bigger picture, then it is easier to see important connections to other groups in the organization. Also, it can be motivating to know what the score is especially if you are part of creating and completing actions that improve the score!

As an Initiating Sponsor, if your workplace has no measurable goals, then power struggles will happen below you because employees will simply have to guess.

See Chapter 2 (p. 31) for Breaking Silos: Part 1.

Potential Benefits and Outcomes

- Goals clarified and refined in all layers of the organization and in multiple dimensions.
  - Plant-wide BLGs, major initiative, and projects.
  - Department-level BLGs and Work Process Goals that support the plant-wide goals.
  - Workgroup level goals to support above goals in Bottom Line and Work Process.
- Cross-group feedback at the lead team level.
  - Identify internal customer/supplier relationships.
  - Clear feedback from department to department on what they need more of and less of in service to their goals.
  - Dialogue across the department to develop actions to address issues.
- An action plan at each level to accomplish better workplace connectivity and achieve goals.
- An aligned organization through dialogue that clarifies goals and raises issues in each work team.
- Clarity on major issues and a plan to address each one, including how each area must interact with each other.
- High level of participation and contribution from all employees, which translates to increased engagement.
- Employees understand the company's situation, department goals, and how their tasks align with the overall goals.
- Highly synergistic process that allows employees to give and receive feedback about major challenges to achieve the goals, create actions to overcome challenges, and implement those actions.

- Workers become engaged and committed.
- Employees are on the same page.
- Fully aligned workplace!

Conclusion

Goal alignment is core for a well-functioning business. The importance of this chapter is the *interactive process used to achieve goal alignment*, rather than any specific mental model about goals. I use the Rainbow Model. I prefer it, yet you can use the balanced scorecard, the A4 from Lean, or any other model. The key is to align employees with their goals *through* dialogue.

Once an employee interacts about the goals in relation to their tasks, important connections are made, and their ability to help improve the organization increases. In 2011 I wrote, "Imagine the power of having each employee understand how their task helps the business overall!" Gallup answered my question by stating, "Employees who strongly agree they can link their goals to the organization's goals are 3.5 times more likely to be engaged."

However, Gallup does not offer clarity between goals and actions. Understanding the distinction between the two is critical (see Appendix D). In other words, I have seen too many examples of goal setting that have no measurable goals. The key is to start with measurable goals, and then dialogue with all employees to build momentum and raise issues at each level of your organization. Employees that are part of such a dialogue have a much greater chance to become productive, engaged employees.

CHAPTER 4

Process Improvement

"To do a contract we need nine signoffs."
"Our prints cannot be released on time."
"For a five-dollar PO, we need five signoffs."
"Our on-time delivery for spare parts is 45%."
"All our shipments are late, and we allow any customer to expedite."

Introduction

These statements are from situations that I encountered over the years. Each points to a work process, formal or informal, that runs through multiple departments or business units within the same organization.

For some reason, the will to fix processes seems less than the will to solve other day-to-day obstacles. Processes that are interdepartmental pose accountability challenges. Where would one even start? Therefore, quick fixes seem easier than systemic approaches that adjust and improve the process for all users. Unfortunately, each fix may convolute the process and let the sponsors avoid holding the few employees accountable who are incorrectly using the process. Continue this path and you risk handcuffing employees, decreasing productivity, and lowering morale.

Quick solutions generally manage individual problems versus systemic solutions, which see problems as symptoms and review the process as a whole. Systemic solutions include strengthening sponsorship, educating end users, and problem solving with clear goals and balanced involvement of the right technical experts and end users.

Many organizations assign people to improve processes who lack a systemic focus. If the process is running smoothly and the end users can easily get what they need when they need it, then all is well. If your situation is typical, then some of your processes may need improvement. How do you determine if a process is running smoothly? My answer may challenge many of you, but I contend that *you can only determine if a process is working by asking the end users.*

Definitely track and measure any process. Best practice is to set goals and improve the process until your goals are accomplished. Likely, once you achieve measurable goals, such as 95% on-time delivery to customers promise date, then the feedback from the internal end users will be positive. Yet, part of the evaluation should be whether the process is user friendly. For instance, if you add signoffs, you may achieve higher results. However, that extra step adds time that employees could use for higher-value tasks. Therefore, include the end user to evaluate the processes and ensure that the focus is on overall workplace improvement.

Create an engagement culture by involving the employees to fix the daily processes that hamper them. When you involve the actual users to solve the problems, you will see multiple gains. First, the process should be easier to use. Second, solving issues raised by the users helps them see how their input matters. Finally, day-to-day problems should decrease, which in turn will increase morale.

This chapter provides a simple way to involve your employees to reflect on a current cross-functional process and apply small fixes to improve functionality. I have used it to improve an order-fulfillment process, increase on-time shipments of spare parts, and reduce errors in the release of prints for a research and design group.

What follows is a strategic engagement activity to quickly identify glitches that restrain a process, develop solutions, and implement them. It is an excellent partner to an expert model such as Six Sigma, Lean, process mapping, or others in that it will expose areas that can be easily solved by the users and those that need an expert model.

Preparation

Preparation for cross-group process improvement is critical and similar to what is discussed in Chapter 2. You must identify and work with the Sustaining Sponsors above each step of the process. I have done this work across plants or departments and/or business units, and each time there were multiple Sustaining Sponsors.

Having the work driven and contracted by the Initiating Sponsor (single boss above all in the process) is ideal, but not always reality. For instance, in a corporation or large organization, the Initiating Sponsor could be the CEO. Likely they do not know they are the Initiating Sponsor or much about the process that needs improving, nor should they. The key is that the Sustaining Sponsors support and drive the employees to reach the goals.

Sustaining Sponsors must have *clarity* and *ownership* of goals to create a successful process improvement. Then they must support and drive actions by providing time, resources, and priority for follow-up until they consistently achieve the goals.

Prepare the Boss(es): Task one is to sharpen the goals if needed. Learn about the goals to improve the process, and coach the Sponsor(s) to get them measurable and precise (see Appendix D). Process improvement must have a measurable goal and time frame to start achieving the goal. Based on the number of bosses and complexity of the organization, multiple conversations may be required to ensure alignment.

Prepping the boss for the opening statement is the same in most meetings (see Chapters 2 and 3 or Chapters 3 and 4 of Volume I).

Include the Right Employees: Those who do the process must attend the event to ensure success, because they know the daily problems. Many organizations have tried to fix processes for years through various means such as mandated new steps. To ensure success, include the real end users.

Interview the Employees: Use the same process as outlined in previous chapters. Work with the employees to review and verify the process steps. It is not always possible to interview employees. It is a best practice, but not a showstopper.

Mapping the Current Process: Map the process before meeting. I have done this two ways. One, write the process on a white board. Two, walk with a user to each area of the process, from start to finish. The objective is to identify clear and distinct process steps to generate data during the improvement session. Perhaps that sounds simple, but if the process has been ignored, then the steps may not be understood.

Facilitator Preparation: Read the following: Chapters 7 and 8 of Volume I for the core triangle in tense moments, plus the concepts of neutrality and reciprocity; Appendix A, The SIPOC Model; all SATA chapters in *SOA*; Chapter 8, Structure; and Chapters 12 and 13 on Decision Making.

Length of Activity: Length depends on the amount of groups in attendance and the size of the process. This meeting will take at least a day, usually the better part of 2 days. If the work process is small, then you may be able to do it in less than a day.

Room Setup: One flip chart and pens per process step. See Figure 19 for the room setup. Tables in a U-shape would also work to start this session.

Core Mental Models/Skills

- SATA (see *SOA*)
- SIPOC Model (Appendix A)
- Victim/Creator ("I" Language, Appendix B in Volume I)
- Behavior Description (Chapter 4 of *FFF*)
- Decision Making (Chapters 12 and 13 of *SOA*)
- Accountability (Chapter 7 of *SOA*)
- Follow-up (Chapter 10 of *SOA*)

Step-by-Step Agenda

1. Opening Statement
2. Introduce Facilitator
   - Introductions
   - Overview process
3. Present Process Goals
   - Manager presents the goals
     - Specific and measurable (if possible)
4. Generate Individual Process Step Feedback
   - Review and verify process steps
   - Present the SIPOC Model (see Appendix A)
   - Separate into groups by process step
   - Task Part 1-generate feedback using SIPOC Model
     - Identify *Inputs, Thoughtputs, and Outputs*
     - Identify *ideally* and *what goes wrong*
   - Clarify group *rules* for working on process step
   - Choose a presenter for each group
5. Group Dialogue
   - Explain rules for dialogue
   - Each process step shares their entire list
   - Capture issues and develop action plan (SPA, What, and By-When)
   - Work systemic issues (SPA, SATA, Decision Clarity)
6. Measurement and Service Standards
   - What will the group measure?
   - Who is the most logical person to measure it?
   - What service standards must be set up?
7. Close
   - Set follow-up date

Agenda Explanation

Starting Room Setup: A large and dynamic activity requires space to allow participants to quickly move around the room (see Figure 19).

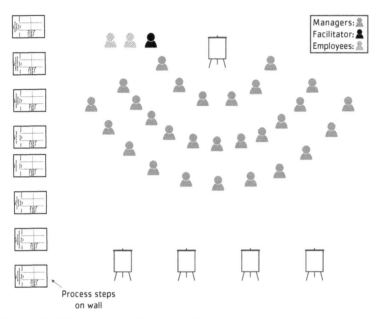

Process steps
on wall

Figure 19 Work Process Beginning Room Setup

Arrange the room with the work process steps visible so the participants can see how the day unfolds. Another option is a U-shape table to start. Make sure participants can see each other's faces.

Opening Statement: The Initiating Sponsor (single boss above all in-volved) or Sustaining Sponsors start the meeting by addressing basic protocols and then introduce the facilitator.

- Review the opening statement section of Chapters 2 and *incorporate as needed for your unique situation.*

Optional Introduction Method: If people attending the event do not know each other, then see p. 16 for an interactive way to do introductions.

Introduce Facilitator: Follow the same process from Chapter 2. Explain that the day is about learning, discovery, clarifying misunderstandings, and problem resolution. Emphasize learning!

Present Process Goals: The key manager shares the goals and time frame. Other sustaining managers can contribute if necessary.

Facilitator task during work process goals: *Opening Dialogue*—same process as Chapter 2, except adjust your questions slightly to the following:
- What do you like about the goals and time frame?
- Anything missing that should be added?
- What are you concerned or confused about?
- What else do you want to learn?

Generate Individual Process Step Feedback: Separate into groups by process step to generate feedback.

Here is the progression to develop work process feedback.

1. **Review and verify process steps**. The group reviews the steps outlined on the wall and answers the following questions.
   - Are they the right steps? Should we add or delete?
   - Are they in the correct sequence?

   The outcome is to ensure enough differentiation of steps and clarity of the process for effective problem solving.

2. **Present the SIPOC Model** (see Appendix A). Explain the SIPOC by relating it to an internal process.

3. **Explain the task**. Use a process step hanging on the wall and tell the employees to complete the chart for each step. In other words, they must write, above the line on the chart, the *inputs*, *throughputs*, and *outputs* for the step being filled out if it is *100% accurate*. Below the line they must write *what goes wrong* at each step (see Figure 20).

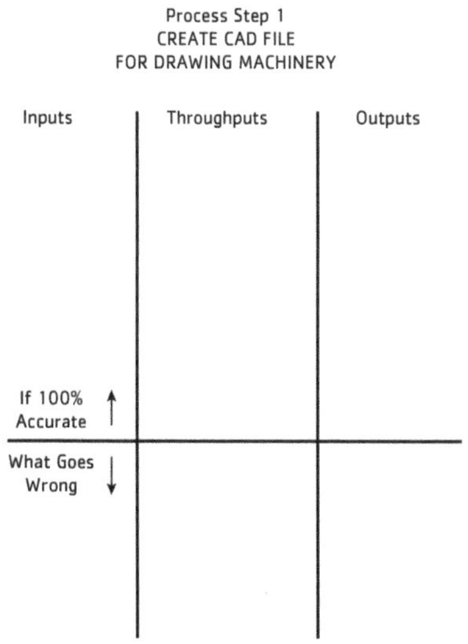

Process Step 1
CREATE CAD FILE
FOR DRAWING MACHINERY

| Inputs | Throughputs | Outputs |

If 100% Accurate ↑

What Goes Wrong ↓

Figure 20 Example of a Work Process Blank Flip Chart

- Ask the participants to go to the process step they perform. Make sure the employees are allocated proportionately so each step is worked effectively (see Step 5, p.54).
- Give the group enough time to do this task effectively. The task could take 45 minutes to an hour. Employees can leave the room as long as you know their location to track and provide the next instructions.
  - Optional: If you are internal, then complete Steps 1–4 in the morning or afternoon. Reconvene the next day to complete the rest of the agenda (items 5–7).
- In 5 or 10 minutes, check in with each group to make sure they understand the instructions.
- Remind the groups to select a presenter for the dialogue.

4. **Translate to behavioral specifics.**
   - After people generate their list, coach the participants to *change any interpretive word into a behavioral specific* (see Chapter 2, p. 20; Chapter 3, p. 44).

Group Dialogue: Start the group dialogue using the same ground rules as Chapter 2, p. 20, plus:

- Start with the first process step and go through the process in sequence to see connectivity and issues.
- At each step have participants focus on:
  - Surprises
  - Perceived differences
  - Unnecessary duplications
  - Input and output mismatches from the last step
- Chart actions complete with SPA, What, By-When, and if others want to help on certain tasks, add a "work with" column to the action list.

During the dialogue portion you are on as a facilitator. Use the same dialogue procedures from Chapter 2 plus:

- Watch for *evil flexibility*—a key person along the process who finds mistakes and corrects them without providing feedback to the person who made the error. Therefore, the employee nor the organization learns.

Measurement and Service Standards: Dialogue about how to measure the process to ensure that it reaches the stated goals. The key is to not add tremendous work to multiple people but rather generate good enough data to troubleshoot problems that hurt productivity.

- What needs to be measured?
- Who is the most logical person to measure it?
- How will it be measured?

After answering the questions, ensure a follow-up process that addresses what is working and not working, and what needs to be adjusted until the process works smoothly.

Service Standards: Some situations highlight the needs for basic service standards when none are available. For instance, a customer service person raised the issue that they had no one dedicated to providing answers on orders of spare parts. Often it would take days to follow up with the customer. A group dialogue resulted in a new process where one person was appointed (SPA) to find answers within 1 hour. The customer service person tracked the new response time and the cause of any responses later than 1 hour. The accumulated data helped solve problems with the process and better serve the customer.

- Include a dialogue about service standards as needed.
- Allow end-user and service needs of customers to dictate service standards.

Close: Apply the same closing process as Chapter 2 (p. 24).

Additionally, ensure the manager(s) set and share a follow-up date. That date should be dependent on the following:

- How broken is the process?
- What dates are on the action list?

A typical time frame is about 6 weeks but that could be adjusted based on the various factors. If this is part of a system-wide activity that includes all groups, then the date may have been preset.

Follow-Up Process: Use the same follow-up process from Chapter 2, except adjust it accordingly to group size. If you have more than 20 people, then forgo rating each item. Instead, break into the process steps, work through the actions and current situation, and then report out. See page 98 for an example planning session follow-up.

Technical Experts

This activity lends itself to using process experts and IT support. An in-house IT resource can often see ways to support the process or improve it through small or large IT fixes.

The process may uncover issues that only a process expert can solve by using integrated ways of thinking, like Six Sigma or Lean. Most processes are complicated by competing needs. After all, the end users (want an easy process), Finance (wants clean accounting), and various other groups have legitimate needs.

Include experts either during or after the event to help solve specific problems.

Success Variables

See the success variables in Chapter 2 and *add the complexity that happens with multiple Sustaining Sponsors*. Best practice is for the boss (Initiating Sponsor), directly above all other bosses, to understand, own, and drive the follow-up. That could mean a variety of things from loose, just checking in from time to time, to more structured, weekly cross-group meetings with all managers. The Initiating Sponsor must remain aware of the progress and intervene if they see slippage in progress. If things are working well, then no different behavior is needed.

Optional Add-ons

This activity can be adapted to meet whatever needs you are trying to achieve by developmental theories. SOCIAL STYLE and Victim/Creator are my two favorites, as previously indicated. If you are trying to improve a process, then find a best practice outside the organization to share and derive implications (see Appendix B, KRID).

This activity may also benefit from John Wallen's The Interpersonal Gap (I-Gap) (Chapter 3 of *FFF*), which adds a frame for how to manage tense moments. If your process owner has an emotional attachment to the process or the separate departments have been infighting around the process, then the interpersonal gap is a nice mental model to hold the participants accountable in the interaction when tension arises. Part of closing the I-Gap is behavioral description, which is key to solving any problem.

The developmental add-ons go between Steps 2 and 3 of the agenda because they frame the day and give mental models to use during tense moments that may arise. However, KRID should be used before looking at the current process and creating actions; therefore, add it somewhere during step 5.

Breaking Silos: Part 3

Cross-group work process improvement is the key to breaking silos. Many workplaces have processes that run across groups that are undefined or clearly not working. For instance, handoffs between design engineers and operations, clarity of rush orders, on-time delivery of spare parts, analytic information about clients, speed of R&D prints released, contracts, and so on.

Chapters 2 and 3 discussed resolving cross-group conflicts and the importance of goal clarity to break silos. Large processes that run across groups, but in less than optimal shape, will only harm intergroup relations and productivity. Use a combination of multiple strategies to break silos, including work process improvements, and stick with it until each group gets what they need, when they need it. Once that happens it is harder to hold on to anger about another group. Yet, if you allow bad processes to stay, they can forever be used as a catalyst for frustration and blame.

Conclusion

Work process improvement is a simple and effective way to improve the connection between steps in a process. It can and should be used to ensure that critical work processes provide the right materials, supplies, products, and services with quality and on time to internal and external processes.

CHAPTER 5

Major Project or Initiative

As a young Organization Development professional, I stumbled upon a research and design group that was struggling to complete projects that launch new products. The business unit was at risk of losing market share. I had just learned the process in this chapter, created by Robert P Crosby, and used it to help them deliver six projects (up from zero the previous year). To this day the VP of Research and Design claims the process as "the" reason they were successful.

Introduction

Major projects and initiatives are part and parcel of organizational life. Almost all large businesses have groups of project managers handling their most critical projects, many with years of experience and most with training in specific project methodologies such as PMI.

Project managers are rarely trained in systems theory and often miss key elements around the people dimension of project management. Those elements are what one may call the *socio-technical* aspects of a project. Socio-technical includes how to 1) link people together who work in different departments (for some businesses that could mean different cities or even countries) and 2) gain clarity of task components, decision making, and sponsorship (as defined in *SOA*). Project managers often create timelines with little interaction with the people who will complete the tasks. They rarely have the assigned resources interact using a group process to analyze potential pitfalls and create actions to overcome them.

Effective project managers must be experts at noticing and managing conflict moments. They must be self-aware and disciplined enough to not slip into their typical conflict pattern or slide into victim behavior as defined in Appendix B of Volume I.

The activity you are about to learn integrates the socio-technical components and has been used in countless organizations often leading to unheard-of business results and huge increases in morale. The activity is best used for major initiatives requiring alignment across your workforce. Examples include furnace recovery in an Aluminum Smelter, research and design projects, software, cost-cutting, major turnarounds of productivity, and more. It will work on any cross-functional project or initiative in your organization if the whole system is aligned to its goals and effective sponsorship is in place and maintained throughout the activity's life cycle. Alignment and sponsorship must be nurtured throughout the activity. That said, alignment is much easier to let slip than to maintain, and the role of key managers (Sustaining Sponsors) are often overlooked when things go wrong (see *SOA* for a reference on how to align).

This activity, similar to goal alignment (Chapter 3) or work team development (Chapter 4, Volume I), will create 50–100 actions requiring attention by the SPAs assigned to each action. Therefore, the Sustaining Sponsors, with appropriate consistent pressure from the Initiating Sponsor, must give employees time and priority to complete their actions or the initiative or project will fail.

For additional reading on this topic, see Appendix N of *CCIO*, titled "A Breakthrough Technology for Achieving Rapid Results in Projects, Initiatives and R&D."

Preparation

Preparation for a project planning session is critical. The key is strong and active sponsorship. Without such sponsorship the work will fail, and employees will blame one thing or another for the lack of progress. Beyond that, this chapter provides a process, from A to Z, that creates a timeline, decision matrix, and clear actions (see p. 101 for an outcome list).

This process avoids the problem created when an untrained facilitator, with lack of sponsorship, brings together a large cross-section of people, raises issues, and leaves with no clear plan of who will do what and by-when.

Systemic Setup

The preparation for a major project is with the key Sponsor. They may be the Initiating Sponsor (single boss above all in the project) or a Sustaining Sponsor in charge of a plant or large department within a corporation. In the latter case, sponsorship is built with the key Sponsor and the Sustaining Sponsors over all areas in the project.

Remember to leverage all forms of structures, formal and informal, that exist within the project. Unions, for instance, have a formal structure that must be honored and worked within to ensure all members arrive with full support from their leadership. Failure to align formal and informal structures will result in project failure or reduced impact due to gaps of knowledge and investment at the event. Remember, success depends on using a large amount of worker knowledge (see Chapter 9 of *SOA*).

It is possible that your scenario requires involvement from outside organizations to effectively solve the problem. If that is the case, then you will have multiple Initiating Sponsors, one in each organization.

If the Initiating or key Sponsor has an active board trying to improve the organization, then that board must understand and support the process or they may kill the initiative by micro-managing the Initiating Sponsor. Two conversations must happen with the Sponsors. First, they need to know, understand, and fully support that:

- This event will likely create 50–100 actions.
- Participants will be required to work on those actions to ensure completion. Significant amounts of time may be required to accomplish the tasks. Because some of them may work in a daily repeatable task, such as on the manufacturing floor, you must allow them time for action completion.
- Many of the actions may appear trivial to managers, but to those doing the work, they represent increased efficiency.
- This event creates a structure (captured on a timeline that I strongly suggest you keep highly visible) to govern the project moving forward and establishes boundaries within key roles. Multiple people may track the project in different places in the organization. Clarity of the governance structure starts before the event, sharpens during the event, and may evolve slightly after the event.

- Resource needs will become clear near the end of the event because the actions will be known and each action will have an assigned SPA. Short-term resources may need adjusting.
- Additionally, systemic issues may be highlighted to resolve.

If you have this conversation with the right leaders and they are not supportive, then cancel the event. However, when this process is supported and sponsored, the gains are immense. If sponsor supported, then you are ready for conversation two: a set of implementation items that must be in place before the session starts.

- *Appoint Project Manager* - The project manager must be aware or willing to learn the socio-technical aspects of project management and be skilled at resolving difficult conflicts.
- *Placement of Timelines* - This session will create several mini and one master timeline that must be visually accessible as tools for dialogue and troubleshooting actions.
- *Set Follow-Up Strategy* - Have a beginning plan for follow-through, formal and informal, before the session. Announce the date at the beginning of the process to increase the belief that the actions will be given priority. Be ready to adjust, as needed, after creating the plan.

Go forward once the structure and sponsorship is in place to succeed.

Prepare the Boss: Learn the Sponsor's project goals, completion date, and follow-up date. Help sharpen the goals if they are not measurable (see Appendix D).

Projects and initiatives are time based. Timelines must be created within the time frame that the organization needs so they do not lose business or market share. When a completion date is known in terms of risk to the organization, then real resource constraints can be managed and cross-department tasks can be synchronized. If no date is known, then it is harder to understand the consequences of actions slipping and projects can delay without awareness.

Include the Right Employees: Those who perform the tasks must attend the event to ensure success. The planning session should include about 50% of the people who work in the area(s) where the project takes place. Why? They know the issues and history of what has and has not worked. Combine the right end users, appropriate technical resources, and managers to ensure the unique situation is properly resolved. Review Chapter 2 of Volume I and make decisions based on need rather than conflict avoidance.

Interview Employees: This is a nice-to-have for this session. However, if the workplace is highly contentious, you may need to meet with key leaders (department heads, union leaders, or others) to broker specific guidelines that allow the session to take place. The structure of this process allows for success even in contentious situations.

Facilitator Preparation: Read Chapters 7 and 8 of Volume I for the core triangle in tense moments, plus the concepts of neutrality and reciprocity. Also read *Strategic Organizational Alignment*, specifically all chapters about SATA. Appendix F, Force Field Analysis and Appendix E, Brainstorming Sequence and Rules are new and core to this activity.

Length of Activity: This meeting will take two full days. It could last longer depending on the number of groups and people attending. I have seen it done with more than 100 people. The process works with an infinite number because of its structure and step-by-step process. Workgroups can learn to conduct this process faster over time.

Room Setup: One flip chart and pens per breakout group. A large room is required with no tables, as participants will move around the room at different times. Post-it flip charts work well because you can use them on any wall if you run out of easels. Start in theater-style seating.

Additionally, you need extra flip chart paper or a large roll of newsprint to create the master timeline. Plus, small Post-it notes, 3×3 inches assorted colors (have at least five colors) and 3/4-inch-diameter (11/16 − 17 mm) round sticky dots; also make sure you have many different colors.

Core Mental Models/Skills
- Force Field Analysis (Appendix F)
- Brainstorming Sequence and Rules (Appendix E)
- SATA (Appendix G, also see *SOA*)
- Behavior Description (Chapter 4 of *FFF*)
- Decision Making (Chapter 12 of *SOA*)
- Accountability (Chapter 7 of *SOA*)
- Follow-up (Chapter 10 of *SOA*)
- Decision Matrix (see p. 86 or Chapter 13, p. 207 of SOA)

Step-by-Step Agenda

1. Opening Statement
   - Measurable Goals, Timeline, and Follow-up Date
     - Dialogue about goals
   - Double-check—Are the right people in the room?
2. Introduce Facilitator
   - Role of facilitator
   - Hand signal to manage group
   - Overview process
3. Develop Workgroups
   - By work problem or department
   - Identify who will facilitate each workgroup
4. Structured Brainstorming—Round One
   - Present Force Field Analysis
   - Use brainstorming process outlined in Appendix I
5. Whole Group Activity One
   - Share top list of restraining forces
     - Assimilate cross-group feedback
6. Structured Brainstorming—Round Two
   - Brainstorm solutions/actions to restraining forces
7. Develop Workgroup Timelines
   - Check action sequence on impact grid
   - Add the SPA and By-Whens
8. Develop Cross-Group Decision Clarity
   - Groups develop decision matrix/stuck points
9. SATA
   - Apply SATA to workgroup timelines
   - Develop communication plan based on learning
10. Whole Group Activity Two
    - Share workgroup timelines, decision matrix, and SATA maps
      - Assimilate cross-group feedback
    - Develop microactions
11. Create Master Timeline
    - Consolidate each workgroup into a master timeline
    - Create resource constraints list

12. Whole Group Activity Three
    - Work the master timeline
    - Participant rating and rework
13. Close
    - Verify structure moving forward
        ○ Clarify roles (Task SPA's, Project Managers)
    - Remind all of the formal follow-up date

Agenda Explanation

Starting Room Setup: See Figures 1 and 2 in Chapter 2 for the initial room setup and the proper arrangement for individual workgroups.

Opening Statement: The Initiating Sponsor (Single boss above all involved) addresses basic protocols; introduces the facilitator; and then presents the goals, time frame, and project structure. Chapter 2 of my first book illustrates an example of presenting clear goals.

> **Plant Manager Gives Project Goals:** "We are currently losing money in the market. It costs us $1.48 per pound to make aluminum ingots and we sell them for $1.36 per pound. If we do not lower the cost of making ingots, we are in trouble as a business. In 9 months, our goal is to reduce the cost of producing a pound of ingots to $1.21."

The Initiating Sponsor must state clear, measurable goals and a time frame for completion. Additionally, the Initiating Sponsor must describe the current situation facing the organization and the likely impact of success or failure with the project to ensure all employees understand the organization's situation. Finally, the sponsor announces basic project structures: the project manager, where the timeline will be posted, and specifics about follow-up.

Facilitator task during project goals: *Opening Dialogue*—Same process as explained in Chapter 2, except adjust your questions to be ready for the planning process.

- What do you like about the project goals and time frame?
- What are your concerns?
- What are you confused about?
- What do you need to know more about?

Are the Right People in the Room? Now that the participants fully understand the problem, have them turn and talk to each other about:

- Do we have the right people or departments represented to solve the problem?
- If no, who should we invite?

Many things could happen regarding these questions. One, you could say yes and keep going. Two, you could say no and have a few people invite other employees. Finally, you could create a list and reconvene on another day because the right people to solve this problem are not present.

Doing this step at this stage rather than before the session, is optional and only done occasionally. It requires an open leader and a unique situation to apply this approach. However, when groups identify additional people to solve a problem, the contribution from the added people is usually substantial.

Introduce Facilitator: Follow the same process from Chapter 2. Include the goal of gaining absolute clarity of tasks that must happen to successfully complete the project on time and with quality.

Develop Workgroups: Here are common ways to organize the workgroups. One, arrange the workgroups before the session by either department, work team, problem area, or another variation and announce them in the meeting. Two, follow the process in Chapter 3 for workgroups of 15 or more (see p. 53). Even If using option one, consider having the participants self-select where they work (see Chapter 3, p. 54, Step 5).

Once the groups are set, have each group pick one person to be the main scribe (i.e., the person who will write the participants comments on the flip chart during the brainstorming session). The scribe still participates as a group member by adding their own items during the brainstorm session and contributing to each dialogue.

Structured Brainstorming Round One: The first round of brainstorming identifies the restraints that must be addressed to ensure a successful project.

Start by presenting Force Field Analysis (see Appendix F); then follow the brainstorming sequence and rules as shown in Appendix E.

This is a key moment because you introduce a structure that must be followed closely or the activity will not work (see Volume I, Chapter 7,

p. 86) You must watch each group closely so they do not break the rules in Step 1 of the brainstorming process. The rules are simple, but critical (see Appendix E). It is my experience that once you succeed in the first round of brainstorming sequence, it is smooth sailing the rest of the way.

The output for brainstorming round one is each group's *top list of restraining forces*. Expect the groups to have 8–15 restraining forces and 2–3 examples of each force. Figure 21 represents two of the 11 top restraining forces created by a group using this process.

Top List of Restraining Forces
Estimators

1. **Lead Time for an Estimate** – 48 hr to 4 Wk (due to scheduling)
   - Workload exceeds skill set (specific people do specific jobs)
   - Job complexity drives longer lead times
   - Errors/input quality create lead-time delays
2. **Input Quality** (received from a customer)
   - Missing/incomplete information (finish wind load)
   - Difficult to read (fax quality, legibility)
   - Conflicts with architects specs and drawings
   - More time to interpret than to quote – too long

Figure 21 Partial list of top restraining forces

The next step, group sharing, helps sharpen each group's list through interaction with the total group.

Whole Group Activity One: Sometimes called a "fair," this is when participants walk around the room and review what each group produced during their brainstorming sessions. The intention is to let people learn and give input so the maximum amount of brainpower is being used to plan for success.

Whole group sharing has two components: the product being shared and the rules of engagement to ensure effective dialogue, exploration, and feedback.

Product for Whole Group Sharing: *The product for sharing is the top list of restraining forces.* Each group has brainstormed items, reduced them, selected the most critical, and added specificity to each force. A normal number is 8–15 forces.

Rules of Engagement for Whole Group Sharing: Cross-group sharing engages the larger group with each individual group to maximize inclusion, influence, learning, and feedback to solve each specific problem. The interaction is structured to help employees remain in a learning mode.

The process is as follows:

1. Each workgroup selects two people to explain their work during group sharing. For the purpose of this instruction, I call the whole group sharing activity a *fair* and the people that stay in their workgroups to explain, *booth attendees.* One booth attendee stays at the booth at a time so the other can participate in the fair.

2. When the attendees are ready and the top restraining force lists are prominently displayed, I announce the start of the fair and explain the ground rules.
   - **The Booth Attendee** 1) explains the restraining force list, 2) learns from the comments and questions of people entering the booth (capture critical feedback), and 3) ***does not defend!***
   - **Fair Participants** 1) learn about the other workgroups, 2) provide input and perspectives, 3) note and share duplicated efforts, and 4) ***do not attack others!***

3. After about 10 minutes I say, "It's time to switch booth attendees. Also, please make sure you go to each group."

4. The Initiating and other key Sponsors participate in the fair and must go to each group to learn and give feedback about direction. The fair ends when the Sponsors have visited all groups.

5. Direct each group to assemble the feedback when the fair ends and do the following:
   - Make adjustments as a result of learnings from the fair.
     - Discuss items people thought should be added or deleted.
     - Discuss any duplications. Either give them to the appropriate group or verify that the duplicating groups have such different contexts that both should work the duplication.

The outcome of whole group sharing one is a solidified restraining forces list that has been vetted and adjusted as a result of the interaction. Also, the interactions with Initiating or other key Sponsors help ensure that the groups are on the right track.

Structured Brainstorming Round Two: The second round of brainstorming identifies *solutions* needed to reduce the restraining forces and *successfully complete the project.* Each group brainstorms solutions. I instruct people to make sure they don't focus solely on reducing the restraining forces. Also *focus on the required actions for your area to be successful.* I reinforce the latter throughout the action selection process.

Participants follow the same process as during round one of brainstorming. The output of this step is the top list of actions needed to complete the project.

During the process of brainstorming actions, one of your tasks is to prepare for the next step, which means making the workgroup timelines. Create small timelines for each group that have the same dimensions regarding dates. Start the timeline at the current date and go about 1 month after the completion date. Turn the flip charts to landscape orientation and use tape to combine enough for the timeline. You can also use rolls of plotter paper for a continuous timeline with no tape.

Develop Workgroup Timelines: Each workgroup uses the top list of actions to make their workgroup timeline. These timelines will be combined to create the master timeline. Each group now works on several small remedial tasks.

Here is the step-by-step process.

1. Number the actions on the list. Choose a colored 3 × 3 inches Post-it note to represent your group, and write the name and number of each action on *two* Post-it notes. Place the two sticky notes on the flip chart with the corresponding action.

2. As a group, discuss the sequence in which the actions should be completed, and *place both sticky notes on the timeline at their completion date.*

3. Check the sequencing of each duplicated action using the impact grid (see Figure 22).

The two dimensions of the impact grid are 1) speed of seeing results (how fast you will see the results when the action is done) and the 2) amount of impact (the results will be high or low). Copy the impact grid onto a flip chart large enough to fit all the extra action Post-it notes.

After placing all duplicate actions on your impact grid, then double-check if they are on the right spot on the timeline.

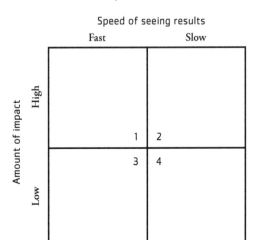

Figure 22 Impact grid

Review the low and slow actions and determine if they are still ne-cessary (see Figure 23). Do not remove actions from the timeline based on their location on the impact grid, but rather use the grid to guide dialogue. Sometime there are items that appear low and slow yet need to remain and vice versa.

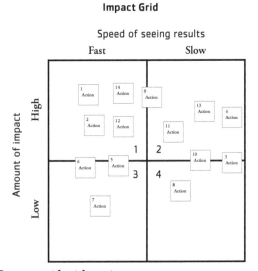

Figure 23 Impact grid with actions

4. Use the impact grid to adjust the timeline sequence.

5. Add the SPA and By-When date to each action.

Determining the SPAs often changes the group dynamics. The By-When is easy because it is where the action falls on the timeline, but the SPA means someone in the group must commit to doing and constantly tracking their particular action. Each action must contain a person's name; that person must be in the room, preferably in the workgroup. If a name is chosen outside the group, then that person must acknowledge and accept the action. Ultimately the right SPA is a decision by the right Sustaining Sponsor, so slight adjustments may happen outside the session. When hourly workers are excited about specific actions, they are usually eager to be the SPA. Whether Union or not, this holds true.

A workgroup timeline is complete when you add the SPA and By-When to each action. Figure 24 illustrates vetted actions and checked sequences.

Figure 24 Sample workgroup timeline

On Figure 24, if you use your magnifying glass, I have written the words "SPA," "Action," and "By-When" on each action. Your timeline for SPA will have a name, the action will be clearly written, and By-When is the completion date.

Develop Cross-Group Decision Clarity: The planning participants reconvene at the front of the room, are given a theory on decision making (Chapter 12, *SOA*), and then each group creates a decision matrix in relation to their timeline (see Figure 25; or Chapter 13, p. 207 of *SOA*).

This critical component of cross-functional projects is often overlooked or misunderstood. Here are a few basics of what I say at this point. "You all have a history here and have had experiences where things get stuck or bogged down for whatever reason. I want you to spend some time and identify predictable 'stuck points' in the project and develop decision clarity for each issue to get unstuck. For each item I want you to

Work Issue Requiring Decision?	Who Decides? (SPA)	Who is Consulted Prior to Decision?	By When?	Who Carries Out the Action?	Who Needs to be Informed?
Approval of Rationalization Criterion	Clive	David, Shari	11/31		

Figure 25 Example decision matrix

choose the best person to make the call. Meaning, if you had to bet on it, the person that would know what will work best in your organization.

In one project that meant that the group chose a person operating the machines on the floor. A common trap in organizations is to think that the highest ranking person should decide everything. That will never work. In fact, for the person deciding when enough promo items had been added to the batch, the group originally had the business unit VP making the decision, six levels above the frontline employee who eventually made the call. Challenge yourself to raise the real issues that have been stuck in the past and make sure that you choose the right SPA."

Further I state, "Please notice that the chart has the category 'who is consulted before the decision.' This is very critical. Being a SPA does not give you the right to be dictatorial. In fact, it is about clarity to make on-time, quality decisions. Therefore, you must consult with those people and learn before making the call. Make sure you challenge yourself to complete at least the first four categories.

Finally, decision stuck points are only as good as the systemic alignment. Therefore, the project manager must help the sponsors hold people accountable to ensure that the decisions are completed on time. The project manager must continually work with the right people to resolve roadblocks. OK, your task is to return to your groups and complete your decision matrix."

The typical output of this step is that each group develops 4–6 stuck points to ensure project success. In project planning sessions of 30–70 people, I normally get 20–40 stuck points.

Apply SATA: Teach SATA and help the group identify their particular SATA role and build sponsorship for project success.

Here are two options. 1) For a new group with no exposure to the theory, give the whole sequence as outlined in Appendix G. 2) For a group with previous exposure, give a thumbnail of the theory and have participants discuss their SATA experiences in terms of what has and has not worked. Finally, focus on creating SATA maps.

Before creating the SATA map and after the SATA presentation, discuss informal influencers in the organization that, if kept out of the loop, could hurt the project's chance of succeeding. Aligning the organization includes aligning formal and informal influencers. Identify informal influencers as part of the communication strategy.

Create SATA maps (see Figure 26)

- Use the *Action List* and *Decision Matrix* to draw an organization chart (map of legitimate authority) up to a single point, starting with anyone who is a SPA for an action on the timeline or decision matrix.
- Identify who is and is not in the session.
- Identify key informal influencers not present.

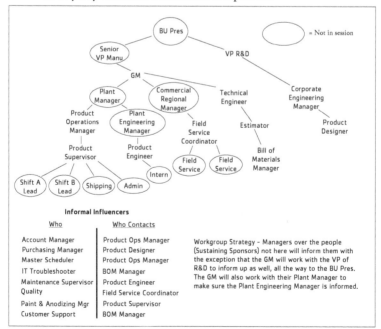

Figure 26 Workgroup Project SATA Mapping

- Develop a list of who will inform the people who are not in the room about the session, major issues and how they will be addressed, task requirements, resource needs, and ways to influence (see Figure 26).

The example is real (titles and roles were used instead of actual names). *The key is to be clear about who will inform the people identified on the chart that are missing* and could impact the actions: either sponsors, targets, or informal influencers. This way your organization dramatically increases its odds that all key players are clear about the project, how it will be implemented, and how to influence (see page 98, Follow-Up Participants).

Whole Group Activity Two: Use the same rules of engagement as outlined on page 82.

Product for Whole Group Sharing: Round two—The product for sharing is the short list of actions, workgroup timelines, the decision stuck-point charts, and the SATA charts.

Beyond learning and giving feedback, make sure the participants:

- Look for duplications and decide if they are necessary. If not, negotiate which group takes which items.
- Look for crucial actions that are missing and must be added.
- Verify that the right groups have taken the right items.

This time the Initiating and other key Sponsors go to each group and pay extra attention to work resources, issues, and duplications.

Each workgroup assembles feedback at the end of the fair and makes adjustments as needed. Each workgroup identifies a SPA for the timeline that will coordinate with the project manager to ensure tasks are completed on time.

Develop Microactions: SPAs for actions in each workgroup develop microactions to achieve their particular action. In other words, each step that must happen to complete the task and By-When. Microactions or substeps ensure tasks get done effectively and are a good double-check for task time frames. Distribute the substep worksheet from Appendix L. This task can also be given by writing it on a flip chart and sharing it with each group when needed.

While participants assimilate the second fair and develop action substeps, build a master timeline big enough to accommodate each group's timeline.

Create Master Timeline: Each workgroup uses their duplicated actions to create the master timeline as follows:

- **Add Actions to Master Timeline**: Place the duplicated actions from the workgroup timeline on the master timeline. Figure 27 illustrates a master timeline representing the names of the four workgroups used in a successful planning session.

  The goal was to solve production issues on a new line in a manufacturing plant.

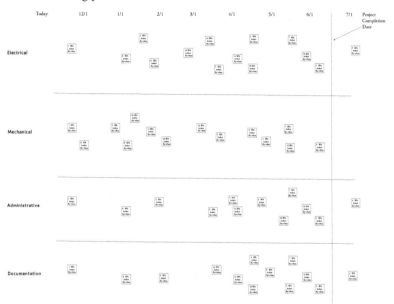

Figure 27 Example master timeline

- **Create a Rough Resource Constraint List:** For each action placed on the master timeline, add a tick mark on a flip chart placed near the master timeline to provide a visual of resource constraints (see Figure 28; taken from a real session).

The resource list is not perfect, as it does not show the amount of work contained in each action. However, this quick and dirty list does highlight imbalances. For instance, Angela has by far the most actions. This chart helps sponsors balance workloads. Sponsors can either monitor closely to ensure Angela succeeds or remove tasks so she has time to accomplish the assignments. Angela was the project manager, so the number of tasks may have been appropriate. The list highlighted potential obstacle nonetheless.

Figure 28 Example resource list

After creating the timeline, prepare the room to work the master timeline (see Figure 29).

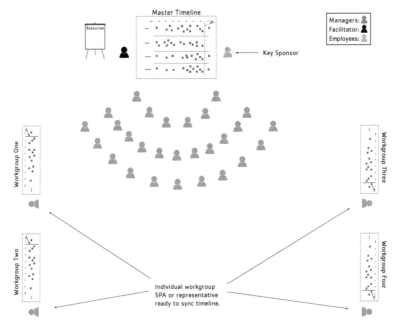

Figure 29 Room Setup to Work Master Timeline

Whole Group Activity Three: *Work the master timeline.*

Here are the basic mechanics. First, an Initiating Sponsor or key Sustaining Sponsor will work the timeline. Second, each workgroup identifies a SPA or representative to adjust their mini timelines per results of working the master timeline, such as different dates or SPAs. Finally, all other participants interact with the sponsor to work the master timeline.

Before this moment, prepare the Initiating Sponsor for this task. The task can be quite intensive. If the Initiating Sponsor is not detailed, then select a detailed Sustaining Sponsor who understands the resources, including the workload and capabilities of those assigned action items. The facilitator must help the initiating or other key Sponsors engage to make key decisions during this process.

Work the master timeline after the room is set up. Each person has a role to play. The person working the timeline goes action by action over the timeline, reading each action aloud. Make sure they go up and down the timeline rather than across each workgroup (see Figure 30).

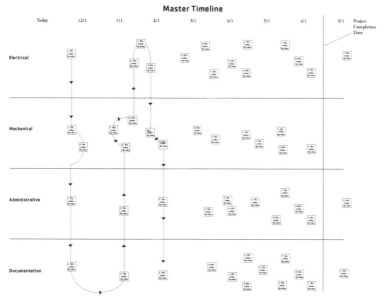

Figure 30 How to Work the Master Timeline

Why? A major task is to catch actions out of sequence with other groups and resolve the conflicts so tasks are finished on time. I conducted a session where the designers said the final design would be done by May. Yet, procurement needed the design to order parts (custom made in tool shops) by April or the machines would not be built by July. This process uncovered the problem, which would have otherwise delayed the project by at least 1 month. Armed with such knowledge of intergroup connectivity, adjustments can be made to keep the project on track.

Participant Roles while Working the Master Timeline:

- *Person working timeline* and the group verifies the actions and resolves duplications, unnecessary actions, alignment around dates, sequencing of events, (eliminates) nonactions, large actions that need substeps created, verify SPA for each action, identify wrong SPAs and SPAs not in room, ensure actions are at the end date (By-When), and if SPA actually does the work (if not, then maybe it is the wrong SPA).

- *People with actions* speak up if a date is out of sequence on coordinated actions or if there is perceived conflicting issues. Plus, verbally confirm they are aware of and will do the actions for which they are the SPA (say "I got it!").

- *Project manager* charts issues and new stuck points.

Your job as a facilitator is to help the process maintain balance. Often the person working the timeline goes too fast or too slow. Here are a few ideas of what to say to address process issues.

- *Moving too slow*: "OK, you're getting too bogged down in details." To the person who is the SPA for the action, "Are you clear about the action and do you accept SPA responsibility?" When the person says, "Yes," then say, "OK, next action!"

- *Moving too fast*: "Wait, you have read five actions and nobody has commented." To the SPA of the last action spoken, "Are you clear about the action and do you accept SPA responsibility?" "Is this action dependent on another action?" If yes, then "What is the other action and is it at the right place on the timeline?"

This process is a total group dialogue to establish a timeline as accurate as possible. During the process use all the interactive skills you have been cultivating throughout this book. Task component clarity of actions and decision stuck points are key. How individual items are completed can be clarified later. Emerging actions after the session must be brought to the project manager to update the timeline.

Participant Rating and Rework: See page 24 and use the same closing process to ask the following:

A. What is your confidence level we have the *right actions?*

B. What is your confidence level we will have a *successful implementation?*

C. Was I *free to influence* the timeline?

D. What is my *commitment* to this change?

Rate each question on a scale of 1–10, with 10 being high.

Consider, based on the scores, having each group discuss the following:

- For A, what actions must be added?
- For B, what areas of implementation are you concerned about that do not have an action to address?
- For C, what did you want to influence that you didn't?
- Do not discuss D. However, if scores were low and you work effectively with the responses to the three previous questions, commitment will go higher!

Assimilate any new actions resulting from this conversation.

Close: Reiterate the next steps, including how the project will be managed. Include the following:

- Read to the participants the appropriate parts of Appendix M.
- Sponsor verifies where the mini and master timelines will be posted.
- Answer questions about next steps.

The sponsor then reminds the participants about the formal follow-up date.

This is a detailed and complex planning methodology. It is critical to have a plan and be able to shift as new situations unfold. Learn the fundamentals of this session and adjust accordingly. Workgroups can learn to conduct this process faster over time. The process typically takes 2 1/2 days to complete. Yet, in one organization, after several sessions we began reducing time and eventually completed subsequent sessions in 1 day.

Faster and quicker does not mean better quality; nor will it necessarily save money. If time is reduced, then make sure you do not skimp on decision stuck points, systemic alignment, and diligently working the master timeline. The objective is to reach business results.

Follow-Up

A successful project requires effective, consistent, ongoing follow-up. Many great events stall because of lack of effective follow-up, thereby requiring extra diligence. The consultant must help the client establish effective follow-up procedures. Effective follow-up has *formal* and *informal* processes (see Chapter 10 of *SOA*). Page 98 outlines a formal follow-up session that should be applied at least once for any major project.

Appendix M outlines the role of SPA of those responsible for an action and the project manager. In each I emphasize that ***this is not a passive role***. The same holds true in aligning key Sponsors to create effective follow-up strategies for any mission-critical project. If leadership is passive, then the chance of success decreases and the probability for blame increases.

Instead, create solid follow-up strategies and continue adjusting until obtaining consistent results. Start by honoring the fact that each organization is different. Therefore, begin with a reflective conversation about how prepared your organization is for follow-up. Here are some potential topics to discuss.

- What is our track record of success?
- Do we have existing structures in which to integrate this project, such as meetings or other communication channels?
- Do we need to create specific ways to manage this project?
- Do we have clear structures to manage conflicts between departments that must work together, or do we need to think about an extra governance structure to work through tension?

Effective consultants/facilitators raise the tough and obvious ways the organization is not working and helps the sponsors create strategies to ensure success. You may hear, "This time we will just have to succeed." Yet, if no different way of succeeding is created, then gently remind them that *the likelihood that staying the same will yield better results is very low*.

To help further develop successful strategies for follow-up, here is an example of how one project manager successfully used informal and formal follow-up. Quickly after the planning session, actions started to slip and conflicts arose around work priorities. As you read further, please

remember to derive implications to your unique situation and only implement what you think will help you succeed.

Informal follow-up- Informal follow-up is the day-to-day activities of
the project manager (overall project SPA) that helps the improvement
efforts stay focused after the initial meetings or event. This person must
have the necessary time to do a thorough job, beyond monitoring from
their desk. Change doesn't happen magically. As in raising a child, there
must be constant monitoring, nurturing, and commitment. If effective
routines are not in place, then expect to fail or be less than successful. The
SPA (project manager) must focus on the following to maximize success.

1. Education and check in with the boss or bosses.
2. Education and check in with the employees (action SPAs).

Task One: The project manager educates the boss(es) frequently regarding completion of tasks/By-When's. The check-ins include upcoming
milestones, critical decisions, and overall progress.

The project manager helps the boss(es) use their time wisely by calling
attention to potential problems before they arise. They help the boss(es)
be in the right place at the right time.

Here are two ways one highly successful project manager accomplished this task.

- First, the project manager created a two-week out list of actions
  and distributed it weekly to the boss(es) of those doing the
  work. This person taped it to each boss(es) computer along with
  notes on:
  ○ Who's doing what.
  ○ What's working well.
  ○ Who's struggling.
  ○ Who needs more clarity.
  ○ Who needs to be visited or called and about what.
- Examples of what the project manager asked the boss(es) to do:
  ○ Praise successes.
  ○ Clarify expectations.
  ○ Reaffirm the project action as a work priority.
  ○ Redirect or refocus resources.
  ○ Resolve conflicts.

Beyond the two-week out list, the project manager also developed daily lists for each key boss to complete, with suggestions about whom the boss might talk to and what they might say. It is always up to the individual boss to decide, yet many like the help.

- Second, they created and used a visual board. The board stood 14 ft. long and 6 ft. high and was located on the manufacturing floor (the project's focus area). The board contained two critical items: the timeline with all actions and a scorecard with updated goals. These items helped the employees see the project's progression and their contribution to reaching the goals.

Creating a visual board is not new for most. The key is how you use the board to educate the boss and employees. Each day the key Initiating Sponsor and project manager reviewed the board and discussed what's working or not working toward achieving their goals. The project manager also updated the board as tasks were completed or changed. It is critical to constantly maintain the board to ensure accurate data.

The board functions to educate and update the boss and employees while showing the employees that the sponsor is strongly supporting the change effort. The objective is to keep the bosses involved and make it easy for them to show up and support or redirect the improvement.

With today's technology, you could create a visual board that is projected onto any wall. The key is to use the board to continually interact. The risk of keeping the timeline in a computer is that it will not be used as an effective interactive tool. I prefer the timeline literally on wall.

Task Two: The project manager educates and checks in with employees at their desk or work area to discuss project status. They walk the floor and talk to SPAs responsible for actions about what is working or not working and what help they need to be successful.

A key part of the project manager's role is to pay attention to emerging issues and listen to employee concerns. The trick is to help the appropriate people manage the issues that arise. Help the boss be aware of the issues or concerns and to take action or give the reason why they won't.

SATA role boundaries are critical (see p. 167 of *SOA*). The challenge for any project manager or change agent is to not act as if they are the boss by answering things that only the boss has the authority to answer, especially anything of substance that requires dialogue for understanding or orders.

Some critical functions of the project manager are as follows:

- Help the people talk to the boss.
- Help the people talk to each other.
- Help the boss engage around the tasks and decisions and agree when they agree, but disagree when they do not agree.
- Use moments of disagreement to work the issues and to refocus the group.
- Assume problems are good and help resolve them in constructive ways.

Formal Follow-up: Any event created around change must have a formal process to follow up on actions that have been agreed upon. Review your current structure and either incorporate ongoing, formal follow-up or create ways to follow up. Consider the following:

- How often should you meet?
- Should there be a mix of different meetings for distinct audiences, such as managers only, across functions or departments that need coordination, or by separate workgroup mini timelines?
- How will you communicate? How often?
- What is the best way to raise issues around slipping actions? Around decisions not being made?

When meeting, analyze the actions to ensure they resolve the problems they were created to solve. Lean manufacturing talks about follow-up in a useful way. Every action has two components that must be addressed:

1. Did I do what I said I was going to do? If no, why or what happened?
2. Was the hypothesis verified (i.e., Did I get the intended results?).

Effective, formal follow-up includes these components and a structured forum to work the data, discuss the current state, and determine the next actions. It is desirable for all players in the change effort to come together and work the data. In a large organization, that might not be practical nor possible, so create ways to ensure that the right people talk about the right things.

One trap is to send a list of completed items to the project team and not discuss results. This approach only tracks your ability to do actions and lacks focus on progress toward your goal. Instead, bring the right people together, have them talk about what worked and did not work, and use such conversations to ensure the actions being completed lead to results.

The above process is a must for any improvement effort. For large improvement efforts, a more structured process must happen to ensure engagement of all parties in the change effort.

Follow-up is key for success in any project. The message is simple. Plan for and incorporate clear follow-up on any change effort or plan on the change effort to not be maximized.

"It's not what you do, it's what you do next that matters."

Reflect on this section on follow-up and use it as to create a strategy that works for you rather than a prescription of exactly how to do follow-up. You may feel overwhelmed. Your situation, time, and energy for follow-up are unique to your organization. The objective is to set up logical and practical follow-up structures, then evaluate and adjust them until you are successfully implementing the project. Keep checking effectiveness along the way. Waiting until the end may be too late.

Formal Follow-Up Meeting

Apply the following process to conduct a formal follow-up meeting approximately 6 weeks after the initial planning session.

Follow-up Participants: *Be strategic about who attends the follow-up.* All first-session attendees should attend the follow-up, plus supervisors and others who must contribute or be informed. Informal influencers, managers, or key influential employees may also attend the session. Also include SPAs of actions, people helping the SPAs, or those who need to be informed about an action. Invite all sponsors (see Figure 26).

Starting Room Setup: Set up the room according to Figure 29. As the participants enter the room, they will see the timelines and begin to orient themselves. Ensure the mini timelines are accessible for each group to review the issues and work the actions. Each group's stuck point lists should also be visible and ready for adjustments.

Follow-Up Step-by-Step Agenda

1. Opening Statement
   - Brief project orientation
   - Brief master timeline orientation
   - Short reminder why this project is critical to business success
     - Dialogue on first three bullet points
2. Individual Workgroup Sessions
   - Mini timeline detailed follow-up
3. Whole Group Integration
   - Report from each workgroup session
     - Whole group dialogue
4. Close
   - Reinforce roles
   - Q and A

Follow-Up Agenda Explanation

Opening Statement: The Initiating Sponsor reminds the group of the specifics and importance of the project. The project manager then gives a brief orientation to the master timeline.

Opening Dialogue: Before any questions or comments, say, "After this conversation, you will be breaking into individual workgroups (mini timelines). But first, turn and talk to the person beside you regarding any comments about the overall project or about what you just heard." After a few minutes, have a whole group dialogue.

Individual Workgroup Sessions: Participants go to their individual workgroups and process their part of the timeline. New people go to the group of their choice or that represents their expertise. Here is the task:

- Listen to newcomers.
- Talk about what has worked, what has not worked, and why:
  - Regarding actions.
  - Regarding decision stuck points.
- Problem solve.
- Add necessary actions.
- Remove unnecessary actions.
- Follow the same process with decision stuck points.

Whole Group Integration: Have all groups reconvene and dialogue about what is being learned. The mini timeline SPA or one person from each group reports on the following:

- Overall feeling (optimistic-excited-frustrated-stuck).
- Any additional actions or adjustments to actions.
- Any actions deemed unnecessary.
- Any decisions to add or delete.
- Any help needed? In what area?

Reflective Dialogue: Turn to the person next to you and talk about:

- What do you want to learn more about?
- What do you want to say or ask?

Dialogue using the same rules you have learned in this book.

Close: The key Sponsor reinforces SATA roles of the participants and answers any lingering questions.

Optional Add-ons

This activity is highly structured and requires no add-ons. However, depending on what you are trying to achieve, you may want to share a relevant best practice from another location. In that case, use Appendix B, KRID. KRID should be used before solving the current situation; add it before Step 6.

Success Variables

This activity requires strong sponsorship and alignment throughout the whole system. A lot is required to be successful. If you skimp on the activity's systemic setup, then the likelihood of success greatly decreases. However, if you have a strong sponsor who focuses on the organization's action completion and addresses ongoing issues, then the results can be almost unimaginable.

Potential Benefits and Outcomes

Of course, the ultimate goal is measurable results. The following list are outcomes of the initial session.

- Master timeline complete with Who, What, and By-When of each action. This timeline coordinates three to five mini timelines.
- Resource constraints identified.
- Critical decisions identified (stuck points) and a plan to address each item.
- Outlined project structure. Clarified roles and responsibilities of the project manager(s) and people with actions.
- Identified "Sustaining Sponsorship" with a plan to keep them informed and aligned with goals.
- Implementation strategy showing step-by-step clarity, including awareness of systemic change principles to prepare the group for implementation.
- Clarity on major issues and a plan to address each one, including how each area must interact with other areas.
- In-depth analysis of each area.
- High participation and contribution from all layers of the organization, leading to engaged employees.
- Highly synergistic process that allows employees to give and receive feedback about the major challenges, actions to overcome challenges, and decision clarity of key issues.
- Defined micro-projects.
- Workers become engaged and committed.
- Employees are on the same page.
- More fully aligned workplace!

Breaking Silos: Part 4

This session, combined with effective strategy (see Chapter 2 of Volume I), enables silo'd employees to work side by side building and executing a successful plan. The structure provided by the brainstorming sequence only allows crosstalk in specific, constructive ways. Highly contentious workplaces have used it to build a plan incorporating all opinions and minimizing nonvalue-added arguing.

Large projects for most organizations are highly cross-functional even if the organization does not have a formal matrixed workplace. They depend on all departments working together to deliver a product or outcome such as reducing waste, cutting costs, and eliminating inefficiencies. This process is perfect for such moments because it provides a structure that allows the whole system to reach across boundaries and work better together.

To break silos you need time, energy, and the ability to stick to your generative power. Combine Chapters 2, 3, 4, and 5 with other components of this book to create the right strategy to break silos and transform into a highly engaged culture.

Conclusion

This chapter outlines perhaps the quickest way to transform a workplace and get measurable results. When this process is combined with the activities throughout both volumes of this book and *SOA*, your organization will reach its desired results.

CHAPTER 6

Software Basics

Consultant: "I love implementing software systems."
Student: "What? You're crazy!"
Classroom: "Bursts into laughter."

Introduction

After training, mentoring, and experience helping R&D and other projects succeed that were stalling in multiple environments, I spent 4 years embedded on an internal project team for Alcoa implementing a large software system (Oracle) at multiple plants worldwide. What follows is a summary of the socio-technical (see p. 73 and Chapter 1) components used to help the implementation succeed.

The results were substantial. Zero missed shipments and no major disruption at any of the go-lives. Additionally, this result was repeated later as an external consultant on three separate projects, including a multiple country go-live at plants in Korea, China, the Philippines, and Hong Kong.

While these concepts are in the context of a software implementation, they are also applicable in most implementations. Adapt them when creating change throughout any organization. A software implementation presents a clear model of a group (the IT team) creating a product for use by another group (the end users).

In reality, many employees in organizations are doing the same thing. They create products used by other groups, yet often miss systemic principles of change, and therefore make similar mistakes that are common during software implementations.

Often with software implementations the stakes are higher. If a software implementation fails that is used to run an entire business (commonly called an ERP system [Enterprise Resource Planning]), then product cannot be tracked, shipped, produced, controlled, nor understood in terms of financial impact. However, with any new process or way of working, or new product, a poor implementation adds stress to the whole system that can mostly be avoided.

Here are common mistakes when implementing software systems that also happen when implementing other business items.

- Mistake 1—let's not tell them anything until we turn on the system and then fix the problems.
  - Instead—educate along the way. *Transparency* and *education* create informed end users. Education is an iterative process. The more informed, the higher probability of effective feedback that enables the right issues to be solved so the organization (or work process) does not suffer.
- Mistake 2—train the managers on a process they do not and will not use; then expect them to teach the end users.
  - Instead—align the managers to the process changes and have them identify the real end users. Then teach the end users and provide support as needed.
- Mistake 3—learn from the users until you are sure about their needs. Then create the system or product and have them start using it.
  - Instead—after you have learned from the end users and created a product, then use it as part of an iterative improvement process. In other words, the end users test the product, raise issues, solve issues, and retest. *Stay in the cycle until the end users determine the product is ready.*

Software Implementation (or Any Change) Basics: Basic systemic principles must be followed for change to be effective. This includes project work, process improvement, or any other activity. This chapter focuses on software implementations, yet the principles apply to all change.

Governance: Leaders must be aware of clarity of authority, which is a key distinction in any project. Otherwise they risk having those who are implementing change overfunction in their roles (see p. 167 of *SOA*). **Who Owns the Change or Project:** Herein lies the critical distinction that once understood holds the key to success.

- Implementation team *owns project execution.*
- Organization *owns project success* and *impact to bottom line.*

The rule is, *own what you can and do not own what you cannot.* To live within this rule, you must understand systems thinking and what is taught throughout *SOA*.

It is easy to think that after creating a project team, you are off the hook and the project will lead itself. If change moves forward without a clear governance strategy that includes 1) how the business will make decisions at key moments with feedback from the whole system, 2) how end-user feedback is used to make those decisions, and 3) how all issues raised will be captured to understand the impact to business functionality, then you are likely abdicating your projects, initiatives, and changes.

Abdicating change increases the probability that change will be driven in a way that is more autocratic than most understand. There is a whole industry built around claiming resistance as the main impediment to change. Instead, align your organization and engage the right people at the right time within healthy boundaries that include clarity of authority. If you do not clarify authority and believe the problem is resistance, then efforts such as a new way to do purchase orders, update financial records, organize client data, improve processes, implement software, update records, or any other improvement will likely be subpar in the eyes of the users.

People working in the effected change areas understand the problems and resolutions from hands-on experience. They know what will and will not work. Yet often they are not given the opportunity nor expectation to be part of the solution. Software implementations solve this because those people are easily identified as the end users. Many other change attempts often overlook end users or do not involve them enough.

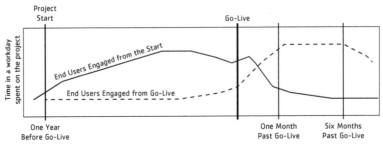

Figure 31 Employee Involvement-Pay Now or Pay Later

However, even software implementations struggle to include enough quality end users. The thought is that it is too costly for the business to remove employees from their tasks. This view creates chaos on the other end of implementations. There is no free lunch. Change these dynamics by setting clear expectations and inclusion of those doing the work to participate with clear boundaries about what they can and cannot influence. Owning the project does not mean that leaders inside organizations must be involved in daily change activities. It means that leaders must be consistently educated so they are ready to make decisions during key moments. Education must come from across the change and be balanced among the project team, the Sustaining Sponsors, and end users. Many miss the importance of obtaining information from end users. That information includes understanding how core issues impact their job function and if they think the solution will help or hurt.

To ensure results, leaders must set appropriate boundaries and engage at the right time. Effective change agents know how to help leaders do this and, if not, they can learn.

Project Governance and Setup: The organization is responsible, aided by a savvy change agent or project manager, to establish project governance that ensures whole system ownership at core moments throughout the project. What follows is the governance strategy used to implement Oracle in 25 locations, across 14 countries, and 4 continents in 4 years.

- **Outside of Project Team**. Create a structure outside the project team to ensure the business understands and manages issues. Use the structure to ensure sponsorship and quick problem resolution.

○ *Location SPA.* This role is a business person near the change area. This person views all processes and interacts with the end users during (and after) testing events to understand how the change will impact each area of the organization. The SPA continually communicates with the location lead team about upcoming events, issues, resolutions, resource needs, and areas that may need business process changes to maintain operations. Throughout the project the location SPA helps translate technical software jargon into real business impact.

- **Inside of Project Team.** Ensure a direct link from each subject area of the project to the core end users with whom they work. This structure must be known to all and used to communicate ongoing needs.

Group Process. Adapt Chapter 5 (plus 3 and 4 of Volume I) to create two sessions.

- **Onboarding Session.** Educate location about the implementation, learn about particular issues related to the location, hear concerns, and create actions to solve items discovered in the session.
- **Location Planning Session.** After user-acceptance testing and before go-live, use this session to educate about go-live, raise issues and concerns, communicate about unique location particulars, and create actions to overcome these items.

Testing Event Feedback. During the testing events, schedule feedback for users to reflect and interact on potential issues as a result of the testing. Use the feedback to educate location leaders and prepare the organization for go-live success.

End-User Advocacy. Gather as much input as possible during software configuration. Listen, paraphrase, and capture each end-user issue. If you can add a "thanks," that is even better. The amount of input generated is largely based on how it is received. Once you capture and understand an issue, use a transparent process to determine whether, how, and when it will be solved. The process must be clear to all, supported by the sponsors, and continued to be taught and refined as the project progresses. If an end user is upset about their issue not being addressed, then add it to the list for an opportunity to be solved.

Decision Go/No-Go. The business must decide if they are ready to go-live, not the IT project team. Clarify decision making when moving from testing to using the system. Most software implementations move in stages from configuration to testing and finally "go-live." Add at least one decision-making process that balances influence from the end users helping to configure the system (by participating in the testing events).

Do not allow the project team to make recommendations about project readiness to the Business Unit (BU) and location lead team without a structure that includes the opinion of the end users. The end users should be able to articulate the known issues to the lead team (coordinated by the location SPA) and their beliefs as to how those issues will impact their daily job function. If they cannot, then they were not involved nor educated enough, and you are assuming added risk.

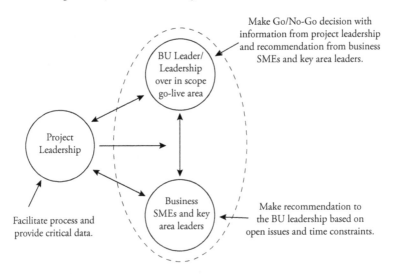

Figure 32 Decision Go/No-Go Structure

Figure 32 is a structure created during a global implementation in one of 22 BUs (SME: subject matter expert).

This process ensured that the software system end users helped decide if their location was ready for go-live. Implement this process and the dynamics between the project team and end users change dramatically into one of engagement and cooperation.

Conclusion

Software implementations and other change activities within organizations can be seamless. The key is clear boundaries of ownership between the project team and business, then diligence by all parties to work together. If you combine this high-level process view with all other learnings in my books, then you can succeed with a wide range of changes.

APPENDIX A

The SIPOC Model

SIPOC stands for supplier, input, process, output, customer.

The SIPOC model is a simple and practical way to analyze interactions between process steps or groups that support each other. The model not only frames connectivity and up and down stream processes but also identifies internal customer–supplier relationships within any organization.

People who supply others with materials, information, or processes often think they should be treated as the customer when they are clearly in a service mode. This confusion adds unnecessary emotionality within a workplace. However, those that receive supplies are not off the hook. It is common that they are not clear about what they want, when they need it, and what shape it needs to be to properly use the supplied product.

After those two dimensions are resolved through a dialogue between those that supply and receive from each other, then workplaces can achieve rapid gains in productivity.

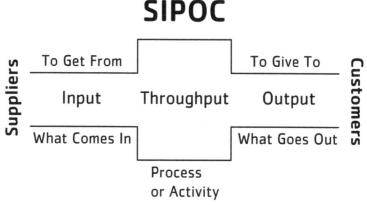

Figure 33 The SIPOC Model

Teaching the SIPOC Model

I teach the SIPOC model in the context of Chapter 2, Group-to-Group Conflict, Chapter 3, Goal Alignment, and Chapter 4 Process Improvement. SIPOC can also be taught ad hoc to help any group explain connections and dependencies in an organization.

Write-up Model (Omit the words "Customers" and "Suppliers")—on a flip chart or white board (or any other means such as PowerPoint), share the model without the words "customers" and "suppliers."

Explain each Term—start with inputs and end with outputs.

- *Input* refers to the materials, information, supplies, services, or any other item you receive from other people day-in and day-out to do your job. Think about it as "what comes in" or things you "get from" others. It includes analysis, advice, and any other information and physical items like materials.

- *Throughput* refers to your daily *process* or *activity*. It is your job, but it could be a task you committed to do or a step in a process. If you are charting a process, then it is one step of that process. However, IT or any group such as HR, Maintenance, Purchasing, Safety, Quality, Finance, and so on complete tasks in service of others. Therefore, their throughput deals with how well they supply internal customers.

- *Output* refers to the information, materials, supplies, and so on that you give to a person or department to do their job. Think of it as "what goes out" or what you "give to" others. In the context of a given problem or activity as noted in Chapters 2, 3, and 4, SIPOC becomes clear very fast to the participants.

Give the basics and then ask the following *critical questions*:

1. **Question:** If I am dependent on getting something from a person or another department to do my job, by definition, what are they?
   Answer—they are my *supplier.*

2. **Question:** If I am responsible to give something to someone to complete their job, by definition, what are they?
   Answer—they are my *customer.*

I do not give the answer unless no one in the group is able to answer within a short time. I prefer to let them hang in silence and grapple with the answer until someone responds. This model is so easy to understand that normally I do not have to wait because they mostly all shout it together.

Potential Process Steps after Giving Theory

1. Generate a list of your suppliers and customers.
2. Generate feedback to each supplier and customer. List could be framed as follows:
   ○ What is working and not working?
   ○ What do you need more of or less of?
   ○ What should be maintained?
3. Dialogue each item and create actions to address.

Conclusion

Simple, powerful, and easy to comprehend, SIPOC is one of the best ways to help organizations change their views of connectivity to service each other more effectively.

APPENDIX B

KRID (Adapt/Adopt)
(Successfully Sharing Best Practices)

KRID stands for Knowledge Retrieval Implication Derivation. KRID was developed by Dr. Ronald Lippitt and Dr. Charles Jung at University of Michigan. Most workplaces use best practices from other workgroups or organizations. Sometimes sharing a best practice has the unintended consequences of creating employees who, instead of learning and adapting a new process, resist the new ideas entirely. This appendix will help you effectively share knowledge and best practices in various settings. Although specifically related to best practices, it is also a great way to recap large events where multiple workgroups have had similar experiences, such as the cascading of goal alignment (Chapter 3) or survey feedback (Chapter 4 of Volume I).

> **History:** When, in the 1950s, Dr. Spencer Havilik experienced the City of Milwaukee *shelve* his water study (which, we now know, would have saved the city hundreds of millions), it was for him the last straw. He met Dr. Ronald Lippitt at the Institute for Social Research, University of Michigan, and with others they founded the Center for Research in the Utilization of Scientific Knowledge (CRUSK).
>
> **Goal:** To research the miss or unuse of knowledge, resistance to the same, and develop methodologies to effectively connect expertise (including research, theory, and successful practice knowledge) to practitioners/appliers who face problems/possibilities that could be enriched by the knowledge.

What follows is Lippitt and Jung's step-by-step technique to successfully share best practices.

Here is a short lead-in to the process:

Most employees can remember a new program imposed by management, insisting that everyone follow the same practice. Many can also remember initiatives (quality initiatives, new business systems) that failed. These failed attempts are called "fads" or "flavor-of-the-month" programs. Why do they fail and what creates success in disseminating good practices so that results are achieved? First, let's review two extremes that guarantee failure.

Become a true believer in the practice and push it on everyone. This is the most popular implementation method. Companies spend mega-bucks on "cookie-cutter" approaches, and training companies flourish by marketing such packages. CEOs often forget the wisdom about managing for results, not for "activities." They count activities—how many people attend quality training or how many crews are now "self-directed"—rather than checking if such trainings or new practices are producing better results in productivity, safety, cost, and quality.

In this extreme, experts on the particular methodology or program being implemented are dispatched to convince, coerce, or otherwise manipulate the resisting parties to conform to the new approach. Consequently, even if the top executive mandated the change, intense resistance and sabotage of the essentials still occur in the new method.

Let the employees decide if they want to adopt the new program. In the other failure scenario, the new practice is suggested and left for individual or group discretion. A few adopt it, some adapt it to fit their needs, and many ignore it.

There is a better way. The key difference is between the words "adopt" and "adapt"—

Adopt = Swallow it whole
Adapt = Fit it to your needs
—and in the paradoxical blending of these two in a unified construct.

Apply these fundamental principles and steps when sharing successful practices.

1. The successful practice must be presented, warts and all, as it is practiced. Presenters of this knowledge must not a) generalize to other situations, b) attempt to apply it for the audience, nor c) sell it. Rather, they must share accurate data with genuine enthusiasm but no exhortations ("This is the greatest thing since sliced bread!") or admonitions ("You must do this or lose market share!").

2. As clearly as possible, measurable outcomes—for which all will be accountable—must be identified and communicated by the sponsoring executives. People will be held accountable for successful results rather than replicating the method.

3. Those receiving the knowledge about the successful practice must demonstrate their ability to accurately articulate the original practice. No arguing. Rather, repeat the words and paraphrase the meanings (i.e., "Here is what I heard you say, and I'm translating it into the following meanings. Do my meanings match your message?").

4. The receivers derive implications for their unique situation. Temporarily accepting the validity of the successful practice, they consider how to implement the process to fit their environment.

5. The initiating executive or key manager, perhaps in the midst of step four, clarifies those aspects, if any, of the practice that are so central that they are not negotiable. Thus, the receivers are clear about what must be *adopted* and what can be *adapted*. While striving for results and not activities as the goal, the executive may have compelling reasons (e.g., standardizing purchasing of costly equipment) to "edict" certain core elements. That which is to be adopted will be met with resistance, of course, which leads to the next step.

6. The initiating executive must listen, stay firm about the core, respect disagreement, and respect anger or frustration if it surfaces. After appropriate airing, they should restate the core (which may have shifted slightly—but genuinely, not as the result of placating but of careful listening) and then the firm expectation that people will follow the leader!

7. Work completion includes selecting and sequencing the practices to adapt, and planning additional training or resources to implement the adopted and adapted practices.

Successful knowledge transfer is enhanced by understanding the adoption/adaptation distinction. One should minimize adoption and maximize adaptation while focusing on results instead of methods. Adaptation is a natural process because 1) situations to implement new practices are unique, 2) communicating a complex practice is likely to have misunderstandings, 3) humans are motivated most when using their own creative juices, and 4) success increases with involvement and belief in the process by those who will complete the practice daily.

Conclusion

KRID remains one of the most practical and powerful ways to share knowledge in any organization that struggles with using learnings from internal or external sources. The process is simple to learn and can be adapted to serve your needs any time. Learn its foundations and add it to your tool kit.

APPENDIX C

Project Implementation Questions

The following was written for a leadership development program where the leaders were working on projects to help develop their skills. I led a session and only asked questions 1, 3, 4, and 5.

I then used my definition of a goal (Appendix D) to help clarify their goals. I discovered that their initiatives or projects had no measurable goals and many had no idea what problem they were trying to solve beyond, "I am fixing a broken process."

Apply these questions to ensure that projects are tied to business results, organizational alignment, task component clarity, and diligence to the socio-technical components of project implementation.

1. What is the problem you are trying to solve?
2. What is the current situation?
   - What is *working well*?
   - What is *not working well*?
3. What are the target goals?
4. What is the completion date?
5. Who is the SPA for the project?
6. Is there a plan stating who (SPA) will do what and By-When?
   - Is there an action list?
     ○ Does the list have Task Component Clarity (Who, What, By-When)?
   - Did you chart potential stuck decisions?
7. Did you chart a SATA map?
   - If so, how are you informing the Sustaining Sponsors about key issues and ongoing resource needs?

8. How often do you meet to work on the project?
9. Is the project completed?
   - Did you achieve project goals?
   - If yes or no, why or why not?

This list helps gain perspective and clarity regarding critical initiatives to improve the workplace.

APPENDIX D

What Is a Goal?

A remarkable number of leaders do not have measurable goals,
which significantly increases the chance of misalignment, in-fighting,
and confusion of direction.

In Chapter 2 of *SOA*, I explain how to transform any statement into a goal. This appendix provides examples to help you solidify the concept and develop clear measurable goals. *The lead in leadership is knowing where you are headed.* This appendix will help you with that clarity.

A goal is numeric and measurable. Many people confuse actions, values, standards, statements, beliefs, and other things with goals. Almost all of these items can be transformed into my definition of a goal. Here are examples from various workplaces.

Example 1—Nonprofit Work Process Goal

Belief: High school students increase their chance of graduation if they complete their homework on time.

Action: I will meet weekly with my students to ensure their homework is completed on time.

Goal: My students will complete their assignments by the deadline 90% of the time.

Once the above clarity is achieved, then track the percentage of time the assignments are completed by the deadline and implement actions to address reoccurring issues. Also track the theory—students completing homework have higher graduation rates—to confirm its success by achieving the process goal.

Remember, work process goals represent *the art of managing* and must be managed and adjusted until you track the right processes that lead to the right bottom-line goals. This example goal is about high school graduation.

Example 2—Manufacturing Plant Work Process Goals

> **Belief:** If we increase our speed of changing products on the line, then we will reduce waste and increase machine efficiency.
>
> **Action:** Set a new standard for product changeovers on the floor.
>
> **Standard:** Changeover a product in 45 minutes.

Goal: Reach the new product changeover standard 85% of the time. Setting and communicating clear goals and holding the Sustaining Sponsors accountable will improve employee behavior to achieve the goal.

If you follow up such goals with a group process and a problem-solving methodology that involves the people who do the work (Example 2, those responsible for changeovers), then the chances of reaching the new goal are drastically increased.

Conclusion

Setting clear, measurable goals is critical to ensure balance in your workplace and align employees to focus on the right improvements. Review Chapter 2, Goals of SOA for a variety of topics on goals, such as the importance of balance.

APPENDIX E

Structured Brainstorming

What follows is a sequence and structure of how to effectively brainstorm. The sequence is practical and powerful and, once learned, can be used in full or in part on an ad hoc basis to help any group quickly manage a list of items. If you have ever 1) seen a group generate a list of problems, yet fail to reduce them to a manageable list of actions, 2) seen a group use votes rather than logic to determine their course of action, or 3) heard a leader say, "Well it looks like we are all in agreement that X is the course of action" without really knowing the differing beliefs in the group and found yourself frustrated and not sure what to do, then the following sequence is what you need. It provides simple ways to resolve such dilemmas.

By learning this brainstorming sequence, you can quickly reduce lists, balance votes with constructive conversations and clear decision making, and get rapid feedback on what options the different members of the group think are the most critical.

Keys of Effective Brainstorming - There are multiple keys to effective brainstorming:

1. Have a clearly defined problem complete with *measurable goals*.
2. Set a *clear timeline* to solve the problem.
3. Build sponsorship and *systemic alignment* of the Sustaining Sponsors to maintain, tweak, and drive the solutions until the problem is solved.
4. Apply a *highly structured process* that balances suspending critical judgment with moments of interaction and using critical thought.
5. Include *the right people*; otherwise, brainstorming will not work because it will have no grounding in reality.

The right people means those who work in the problem area you are trying to solve (see Chapter 9 of *SOA*). Combine them with enough technical experts and managers to quickly solve problems and eliminate guesswork about the best approach. Proper brainstorming generates quick ideas and effective dialogue.

Popcorn-style Brainstorming Often Does not Work - If group brainstorming occurs without a clear structure, it can heighten negative group dynamics. This type of brainstorming, sometimes called "popcorn," is the standard used by most businesses and groups in the United States.

It goes like this. The leader says let's brainstorm some ideas, and the participants start giving suggestions. Each suggestion may or may not elicit a response by other group members. Often a group member or two makes negative statements about what others "storm," which has the likely effect of stopping some of the participants from continuing to give their opinion. Also, often those who give ideas considered positive by other group members get rewarded whether or not their idea has clarity or validity. These groups often either cower to the most dependent or play to the most extroverted members. Shy or introverted members are given a pass even if they are sitting on brilliant solutions that could solve the problem. From a neurological perspective, this type of brainstorming has the unintended consequence of activating the amygdala or reaction center of your brain, which causes flooding of the brain and can trigger fight or flight behavior in group members. While this style of brainstorming is quick and simple and can yield results depending on your environment, it does not work if the environment is hostile or unsafe.

There is a better way to brainstorm based on years of trial and error and in the applied behavioral sciences. The key is clear structure at each step and effective facilitation to ensure dysfunctional group dynamics do not hijack the process. Most have never heard of or seen this type of brainstorming. If you brainstorm without using the five keys mentioned earlier, it will likely fail regardless of the volume of ideas. Instead, determine what must be solved and build sponsorship. Then assemble the right people and follow the structure in this appendix.

More about the Right People - Brainstorming is only effective if you include the right people. Using a solid structure is important, but it is not enough. Data generated is only as good as the people generating it.

The fifth sequence of brainstorming, specificity, will verify if you have the right people. If the group cannot specify any items beyond high-level judgments, then they are likely not the right people.

Who are the right people? Those closest to the work are required to solve the problem. You cannot brainstorm issues about roadwork without anyone who has actually built roads. You cannot solve problems with order accuracy without the people who input the orders into the system and so on. Before starting any process, make sure the right people are in the room. If you do not, and the brainstorm session does not work, please do not blame it on brainstorming!

The following sequence and brainstorming rules were developed over many years and can be used in part or whole to help a group reach a specific result. Read the entire sequence to ensure comprehension. Each step of the sequence is critical and has different rules that help facilitate that stage of the process. Once you understand the sequence, it is easy to recognize people who are stuck because they are doing a task that is out of sequence. Then redirect them to their current task to get the group back on track. The process generates the outcomes, and each step is part of a whole.

This sequence is integrated into Chapter 5, Major Project or Initiative. As you revisit that activity, please note the success or failure of such an initiative is grounded in the systemic alignment, overall sponsorship, thoughtful selection of all layers, and especially effective follow-up. Brainstorming in and of itself is just another tool. When something fails, make sure you correct the systemic issues. The tools are rarely the problem.

Here and Now - Brainstorming using a structured process helps people focus on the here and now of a task. Many will want to jump to other steps. The facilitator helps the group focus on the current task and ensures an effective brainstorming session.

Room Setup - One flip chart and flip chart pens per group. Post-it flip charts work well because you can use them on any wall if you run out of easels. The brainstorming process requires participants to sit in a half-circle around a flip chart. Plus, three-fourth-inch-diameter (11/16-17mm) round sticky dots. If you do not have sticky dots, then people can use flip chart pens to multivote.

Beginning Setup—Before the session starts, write the five steps (as stated below) on a flip chart and the Step 1 rules on a separate flip chart (not visible). If I combine this process with Appendix F, Force Field Analysis, then I have part of that theory ready on another flip chart.

Structured Brainstorming Sequence

1. Brainstorm (generate)
2. Clarify
3. Multivote
4. Select
5. Specify (give specifics of each)

Explanation of Structured Brainstorming

Sequence (Rules and Tips)

1. Brainstorm (generate)

The first step of brainstorming is the generation phase. This process has strict rules to ensure equal participation and eliminate crosstalk. I begin by writing a short form of the rules on a flip chart or white board. Yet, I fully explain each rule.

Step 1 rules

- Take turns.
- One idea per turn. Say "pass" if you have no idea and continue the activity until all have said "pass."
- Say anything that comes to mind (in short phrases or a few words).
- Recorder writes down *exactly* what is said; no editing. Clarity will come after brainstorming is complete.
- Do not discuss ideas when they are offered.
- No evaluations or judgments, positive or negative.
- Repetition is OK.
- Go for quantity, not quality or accuracy. Those are the later tasks.
- Have fun!

The generation phase of brainstorming is intended to tap into the creative right brain and foster spontaneity. Do not allow linear thinking, such as reading from a list. However, if people seem stuck, have them separately take a few quiet minutes to make a list of items to add to the brainstormed list. Then proceed per the rules.

If there is only one group, then I am the scribe and facilitator. If there are multiple groups, like in Chapter 5, then I ask each group to pick a scribe and follow the process very closely, especially in the beginning. With multiple groups, I use extra diligence to ensure they follow the rules during Step 1 of the brainstorming process. The rules may sound simple, but they are critical and volunteer scribes can easily break them.

Here are some common behaviors and what I say during this stage.

- **Situation:** A group member is *thinking* instead of giving a brainstorm item.
  - ○ **Response** - I say, "Pass, go to the next person. Do not worry. We will go around the circle multiple times until all ideas are on the chart."
- **Situation:** A group member comments, either saying, "Good idea" or something critical after a member gives a brainstorm item.
  - ○ **Response** - I say, "See how tough it is to not crosstalk? Try and be disciplined and stick to the rules. Don't worry, you will be able to discuss each item during the "clarify stage."
- **Situation:** The scribe (or facilitator) asks for clarity of the brainstormed item.
  - ○ **Response** - I say, "This is not the time to clarify; it happens during the next step. Stay in the generation phase."

OK, you get the picture. I have, on rare occasions, had to remove the scribe or get the sponsor to help the group stay on task. If you follow the brainstorming rules, then even groups in serious conflict can move through this process. If the structure is not followed, then the session will break down.

Generation Phase Tip. Number each brainstorm item as you go. If you stick to the rules, then multiple flip charts could be filled with items. I have seen groups go well over 100 items. The next segment is clarification. Numbering each item helps the clarifying stage become much easier.

2. Clarify

The second brainstorming step is the clarification phase. Your reward for generating well is that your task to clarify is a larger one. I begin the phase by writing the words ASK and TELL on a flip chart or white board, and then I explain each word.

Clarifying is not a linear task because not all items require clarifying. The goal is to understand the items good enough, as quickly as possible, which will aid the next step of the process (multivoting).

Step 2 Rules
- No arguing the merits of any item.
- Go to items about which you are curious and ASK what they mean.
- Go to items that you want others to be clear about and TELL them (elaborate as needed).
- Clarify until the group is clear enough to move to the next step.
- Do not go straight down the list and clarify each item.

Remind the groups that the goal is to be educated enough to vote on the items you believe are the most critical to solve your problem. Help groups that are struggling to speed up and groups that finish quickly to re-examine vague items.

Clarity phase tip. If you have multiple flip charts of generated items, number each flip chart somewhere near the top. Address one flip chart at a time until you are clear enough, and then move to the next one.

Do not allow people to combine items, as this happens during Step 4. Items might be combined that will not make the final list. Therefore, wait until the time is right.

Finally, if groups are not clarifying words like "teamwork" or "communication," then start asking about the meaning. High-level judgments cannot be solved and some words seem to go unchecked even though they mean multiple things to multiple people.

3. Multivote

The third brainstorming step is multivoting. Multivoting creates a visual of the group's opinion of which items are the most critical to solve. It also balances introverts and extroverts because all participants vote, even if they have not been talking much during the session. However, multivoting is not the final selection, which occurs during Step 4. Final selection must be made during a group dialogue with the goals of the session in view.

Step 3 Rules

Count the total brainstormed items and give roughly 20% of sticky dots to each person who is part of process. If 100 items were generated, then each person gets 20 dots and so on.

- No talking while placing the dots (or campaigning for your favorite!).
- One dot, per item, per person.
- Must use all dots.
- You cannot place all your dots on one item.

Multivote phase tip. Multivoting only takes a few minutes. Prepare your sticky dots about halfway through the clarify step (Step 2). This task is manual and can sneak up on you if you are not ready.

4. Select

The fourth brainstorming step is the selection phase. During selection, employees *voice their opinions* and *think* through which critical items must be addressed to help solve the problem.

The selection process produces the top list of brainstormed items. In other words, the group generated a large list in Step 1 by suspending critical judgment and then clarified the list during Step 2. They shared their opinion nonverbally in Step 3, and now must reduce the overall list to the ones they think are mandatory to solve the problem. The selection process includes dialogue that allows crosstalk, hopefully with curiosity about differences if one person thinks an item is critical and another does not. During this dialogue, *the goals should be visible and used to vet the actions chosen.* Also, the group's sponsor must be present or get significantly involved in some way.

Step 4 Rules

- Multivotes are used as a stimulus, yet not as final say.
- Group decides top items through a dialogue.
- Crosstalk is now allowed and important to learn about differences.
- Items with high votes should not necessarily be chosen; sometimes items are popular yet won't make a real difference.
- Items with no votes should not necessarily be discarded; less exciting actions are often key to being successful.

Considerations

- Actual resource constraints of group.
- This is a consultative process that gives the employees a lot of influence. Yet, of course, the boss has the final say as to whether or not to support the results. Some potential traps for bosses are saying yes when meaning no, or saying no to items in which the group has a heavy investment.

Output—A list of 8–15 items with space between each one to add specificity (Step 5).

Select phase tip. If groups struggle to create a list, then they can start with the items with the most votes and whittle it down from there. The goal is to engage their brains as to which items are the most important. Yet, some groups have a hard time looking beyond the sticky dots.

5. **Specify (give specifics of each)**

The fifth brainstorming step is to specify each item, which is a critical and often ignored step. Each selected item must have one or two "behaviorally specific" examples for clarity. The litmus test is whether you could tell ten people the description and, if they were filmed in another room, they would all do the task basically the same way as shown in the video.

Once you achieve specificity with analysis, then creating specific actions to solve the problems becomes much easier (see Chapter 2, Figure 3).

Conclusion

Brainstorming does not solve all your problems. However, when done right it is a powerful tool to quickly analyze a situation and generate solutions to solve problems. Include systemic alignment around the solutions, and only use brainstorming in the right situation. Brainstorming, like many tools, has been overused in some organizations instead of selectively used at the right moment for the right type of issues. Chapter 5 is an example of how to effectively use this process.

APPENDIX F

Force Field Analysis

This appendix provides a simplified version of Force Field Analysis by Kurt Lewin. Lewin is known as "the practical theorist." This theory applies to many situations. I use it when problem solving or to aid in project or major initiative planning. Lewin pulls from physics to provide a simple frame for any problem. Figure 34 is a graphic of the theory and what follows is how to present it.

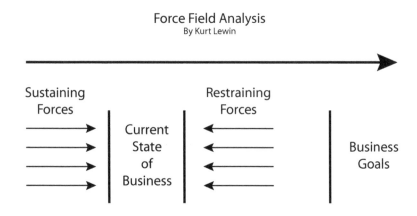

Figure 34 Force Field Analysis

Presenting the Theory - I use the following sequence to present the force field analysis.

Write the words "current state" on the center left of a flip chart with lines on either side. Then draw another line on the far right of the chart and write the words "business goals" on the far side of the line as shown in Figure 34. Then say this theory states that any situation is held in place by two forces. On this side (draw several arrows on the left of the current state) are the sustaining forces and, as most of you know from physics that for each force there is. . . I normally remain quiet and let them answer. Ninety percent of the time they say, "An equal and opposite force." Then I say, "Exactly." Lewin calls those forces "restraining forces."

Most people push harder when creating change and thus, inadvertently, create more restraining forces. Lewin claims by pushing harder, there may be initial movement toward the goal, yet the whole system will always push back to a state of equilibrium. (He calls the current situation a state of quasi-stationary equilibrium.)

Instead, create real change by identifying and reducing the restraining forces. Then the whole system will move toward the goal.

Your task is to brainstorm restraining forces that will keep this (project, problem, initiative) from being successful.

Recap of Basic Principles

1. Any state is held in place by forces that are pushing and pulling.
2. For every sustaining force, there is an equal and opposite restraining force.
3. Reinforcing and increasing sustaining forces or adding new sustaining forces will create more resistance and new restraining forces.
4. If you push harder, you may slightly move the current state, but it will always move back.
5. Change happens by reducing the restraining forces. Reduce the restraining forces and the whole system will move toward the goal.
6. Certain driving (sustaining) forces can be strengthened as long as focus remains on reducing restraining forces.

A few more words on restraining forces

By definition, a restraining force is anything that keeps you from reaching your goal. The following categories help participants think of restraining forces in their workplace.

- **Interpersonal:** Something you see happening between people at work.
- **Psychological:** Fear that I won't understand the new process and therefore resist it.
- **Group dynamics:** Group norms; how the group works together.
- **Socialization:** This is how we have always done it. For example, "We have always used this pecking order."
- **Organizational:** Larger plant issues; physical distance.
- **Community:** Community aspects that might hold us back.
- **Technical:** Part of the machine that doesn't work or knowledge of process.

Don't worry about explaining the categories perfectly, as participants will apply their learnings accordingly. This helps people think a little differently and get the creative juices flowing.

Conclusion

Force field analysis helps gain clarity and direction on items that are often overlooked when managing large projects or initiatives. It is an excellent frame for a brainstorming session. Use this theory in such moments or when people are pushing rather than understanding what is limiting the goal from being successful.

APPENDIX G

SATA Theory Presentation

Understand and live by SATA principles; then engagement
and business results suddenly become attainable.

SATA is a major part of my first book and a critical model to help organizations align their workplace to successfully complete projects and implement other major changes. What follows is how to apply the theory during a work session. To understand SATA deeper, read *SOA*. If you think it's easy, please pause and consider that you may be misreading it. Many organizations use SATA language, yet many, if not most, misuse the concepts and therefore miss its full benefits and powerful clarity.

On page 78 of Chapter 5, Step 9 is SATA. This appendix explains the full presentation. However, only present what is needed to align the organization. In fact, completing each step would not be practical during a project planning session. Yet, understanding the core components to align project tasks within the authority structure of the organization is a critical step toward project success.

Step-by-Step Instructions

Step 1: Introduce Theory. Facilitator says, "Sponsor/Agent/Target/Advocate is a theory created by Darryl Conner and popularized in his book, *Managing at the Speed of Change*. Conner worked with Robert P Crosby and they differed on some critical key points. The following is Robert P Crosby's version of the theory, and I will highlight where Conner and Crosby disagreed.

This theory is *an analysis tool* for when daily tasks are stuck between two work teams or when planning a change (large or small) that runs across work teams or departments. It is important to understand that SATA is *not* a new program. You can train employees in SATA, but it is most powerful when applied toward complicated or confusing scenarios. SATA is a systemic theory of change derived from family systems theory and, in my opinion, paints a picture of reality in all organizations."

Step 2: Prepare Participants for the Theory Session.

- Tell the participants, "Get with like-minded people and choose a struggling, cross-functional situation. The scenario must be current and real. You can work in pairs or with several of you using a flip chart and wall space." Deciding whom to work with and arranging their work space may take a few minutes. Pairs or individuals can use a large note pad turned on its sides (i.e., landscape view). To save time, meet beforehand to prepare the participants and help them identify scenarios.

- If performed during a project planning session (see Chapter 11), then use the SPAs for each action in the mini timeline that was already determined to create your chart (see Task 1).

- Write on a flip chart (or have it already written),

Task 1—Chart a Work Scenario.

Chart a current work scenario, starting with all who have tasks and end users of the product (if applicable). Then draw the legitimate map of authority up to a single boss over all employees charted (see Figure 35 or Chapter 5, Figure 26).

I tell them the task and add, "If you create something that people in another department will use, then they must be part of this chart. If this requires charting everyone in your business, then pick a challenging department(s), identify who has tasks or will use the product in them, and build the chart up from there." I also say, "You may have multiple charts if your scenario involves an outside agency. Chart the person you work with at each agency, and draw the chart up to one person in that organization. Do not define the project or goals; just identify the players and chart the legitimate map of authority (see Figure 35)."

- Continue the theory after everyone completes Task 1. Some will finish sooner than others, but it is better to wait rather than confuse people.

Figure 35 SATA Charting Example

The bold boxes represent people with tasks.

Step 3: Introduce the Four Key Roles. With the words visibly written in Figure 36 on a flip chart, I have the participants sit in pairs throughout the room (assuming you have a large space without tables; otherwise, manage the room the best you can). Then I say, "Whether you are aware of it or not, there are always four key roles at play in every organization. You are always in at least one role and can simultaneously be in multiple roles. However, you can only be a Sponsor if you have direct reports. In fact, one thing I love about this theory is that it is definitional. In other words, you can always analyze your situation through this lens as long as you understand the definition of each role. The roles are as follows:

Sponsor
- Sets (or approves) the goals
- Provides the resources (time, money, people, training, equipment)
- Sets expectations
- Consequence management

Change Agent
- Facilitates change (or tasks)
- Educates (Sponsor, Target)
- Leverages expectations
- Confronts behavior and raises issues
- Helps sponsor "sponsor" and helps targets "be direct"

Advocate
- Has idea
- Must clearly articulate
- Identifies correct Sponsor
- If "no" must let it go

Target
- Carries out actions (or daily tasks)
- Raises issues
- Supported from Change Agent
- Gets direction from Sponsor

Figure 36 SATA Four Key Roles

The *Sponsor* sets or approves the goals, provides resources (time, money, people, training, equipment), sets expectations, and is the only one to apply consequence management. Sponsors either sponsor well or poorly (or somewhere between that continuum) for any given item trying to be accomplished.

The *Change Agent* helps facilitate the change or daily task. Their job is to educate, which is challenging for most agents. They must educate the right sponsor and targets. They help the Sponsor understand key moments, clarify decision making, and drive their change. They help the target raise issues directly and appropriately to the sponsor or within the boundaries of the situation. They also leverage sponsorship, which I will address later. Furthermore, the change agent must confront behavior outside the *boundaries set by the sponsor* and continually clarify those boundaries.

The *Target* carries out the actions or daily tasks. They receive direction from the sponsor and support from the change agent. Their big challenge is to learn how to raise issues appropriately.

The *Advocate* has an idea to change something. Have you ever wanted anything different at work? (Normally I say that while raising my hand and all in the room raise their hand.) If yes, then you are an advocate. Your task is to clearly articulate your idea, in a nonblaming way, to the right sponsor. Advocates often talk to the wrong people (sometimes for years) because they do not systemically identify the right sponsor. After finding the right sponsor, clearly articulate your idea to them and then allow one of two things to happen. First, the Sponsor may get excited and want to immediately implement your idea, which will likely turn you into a change agent. If that is the case, then you must *stop selling* the idea and start helping to implement (selling predictably causes resistance). Once bought "describe," don't sell. Second, if the Sponsor says no, then you must let go, which perhaps is the toughest task of all. Only mention the idea again if there is a change of sponsorship or the situation has changed so much that your idea seems appropriate (be careful in the latter situation to not oversell). Many advocates struggle with the second option and, consequently, create tension with themselves and the organization."

Step 4: Experiential Exercise. I use experiential learning to illustrate a key systemic dynamic related to SATA. I start by saying, "OK, in your pairs I want you to face each other and letter off, Person A and Person B. Ready? Now, Person A, I want you to change something about Person B. It should be something small like how they are sitting, holding their pen, and so on. Go it? OK, I want Person A to plug your ears (look and make sure all are doing it)." Then I say in a soft voice so the Person A's cannot hear, "Person B, your job is to resist at all costs. Got it?" Then I wait for acknowledgment and use my hands to motion to the Persons A's to un-plug and I say, "Go!"

I then watch the show for several minutes. At times I push Person A by saying, "Come on Person A's, I want you to work harder!" Then, eventually I say, "Cut, now, debrief!"

Debrief Questions

- How did it go?
- Person A, what did you do to try and change Person B?
- Person B, how did you resist?

I allot a few minutes for the pairs to debrief and then say, "OK, I would like to hear what happened. First, Person A, what did you do?" I listen and perhaps summarize the story by saying things like, "You tried to tell them the benefits of sitting with better posture."

After listening and summarizing the techniques used to attempt to change the other and the ways in which participants resisted, I ask, "Was anything about this dynamic familiar to you in your workplace?" I let them grapple a bit. Almost all eventually nod their head yes. Then I ask, "What was missing for successful change to occur?" I then allow for a long pause, resulting in some common answers.

"I was not compelling enough."

"I should have talked about rewards."

"They did not get the benefits."

After hearing various reasons, I tell them, "I presented a scenario and deliberately gave competing priorities. In other words, *sponsorship to accomplish the task was missing.* Managers do their best to accomplish their assigned work. *Most misaligned situations are unintentional.* That is, one employee's boss places high priority on a certain task and another employee's boss places high priority on a different task that conflicts with the other task. The tension is felt at the level of the employees who are doing their best to achieve their bosses' priority. Yet, the priority conflict may or may not be solvable at the level of the two employees. The systemic conflict is between the two bosses."

Step 5: Explain Each SATA Role in Action. I return to the theory and complete the definitions using work examples by diagramming each role on the flip chart.

I write the following scenario while saying, "Let me show you an example from the manufacturing world that applies to any situation." Depending on where I am working, I use the most relevant situation possible to illustrate these concepts. All organizations have employees within departments servicing other departments. For example, in a nonprofit I recently used the example of Marketing trying to get stories from the direct service staff to promote the program. This appendix uses a standard go-to, which is maintenance to the production floor. This also works well with Quality or any other group that services the floor.

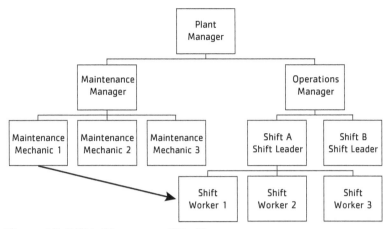

Figure 37 SATA Diagram on Flip Chart

Standing next to the flip chart with the diagram displayed like Figure 37, I say, "So, this maintenance person (Maintenance Mechanic 1) is going to the floor to work with this shift worker (Shift Worker 1). By definition, what is the maintenance person's SATA role?" I pause, hear the answer, and correct it if it's wrong. Then I say, "By definition, what is the shift worker's SATA role?" Then, I write the answers on the flip chart.

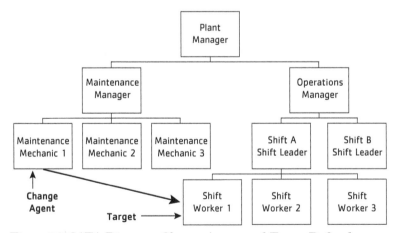

Figure 38 SATA Diagram, Change Agent, and Target Defined

I then ask perhaps the most critical question. "Who is the Sponsor of the work? That is, who is *the Sponsor where the work is taking place?*" I let them grapple until I get a few answers.

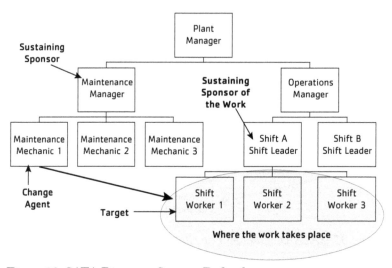

Figure 39 SATA Diagram, Sponsor Defined

I then add the Sponsor and say, "The critical factor that many miss is that *you can only sponsor your direct reports.* That is where Conner and Crosby disagreed. The boss of the maintenance mechanic sets his work standards and is indeed a Sustaining Sponsor. However, *if that mechanic is on the floor,* whether they are aware of it or not, then the *shift leader is their sponsor at that moment. The shift worker listens to their boss no matter what (with few exceptions), and if their boss is telling them to do something different than what the maintenance mechanic wants, the shift worker does what their boss, their sponsor, wants.* Most view those moments as personality issues (i.e., the workers on the floor are difficult, yet really such moments are systemic issues). The goal is to solve the issue on the floor (i.e., through communication between the maintenance mechanic and shift worker). If not, then escalate the issue to the appropriate level. Most miss this critical distinction, and most change agents undereducate the Sustaining Sponsors where the work takes place.

Imagine these two scenarios and choose the one in which you would want to work. First, you arrive and the employee is busy doing something else and does not want to do what you ask. Second, you arrive and the employee says something like, "Glad you are here because my boss is eager to get this done. My boss told me to inform them of any issues once we are done."

Which scenario would you prefer? I hope it is as obvious to you as it is to me; the second scenario is ideal. It may be rare that scenario two would be so overt. However, consider that when things are working well, sponsorship is in place; when things are not, it is out. *A change agent must leverage the change* by either 1) directly working with the sponsor over the impacted area or 2) having your boss work with the sponsor to align the whole system. This is not rocket science. All bosses need to know the task you are trying to accomplish: why, how long it will take, how to manage issues, and how to decide critical items.

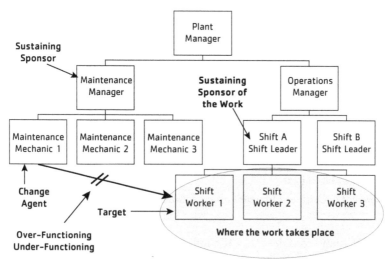

Figure 40 SATA Diagram, Over-Functioning and Under-Functioning

The problem is that most are unaware of these dynamics and, in fact, change agents often do not recognize their SATA role. When unaware change agents get so-called resistance from a target, the risk of dysfunction goes in one or two directions. First, they could *overfunction*, which essentially means *acting "as if" you are the other's boss* by saying *you must do this*, which invites a fight or reactivity because employees always know who is their boss. Second, and even more common, is what I call *underfunctioning*, which means the task is not completed nor raised to manage the systemic issues. The mechanic may say, "No problem, I will come back tomorrow." Then, tomorrow the same thing happens and they remain in the cycle without raising systemic issues or completing the task. In fact, the task or activity may not be critical, but the employee will never know without the clarifying conversation. I believe underfunctioning happens in organizations more often than overfunctioning.

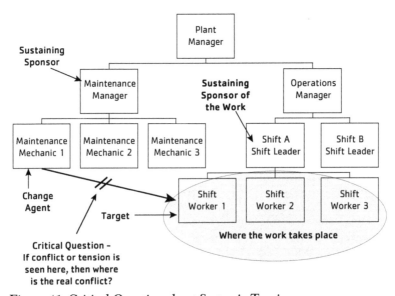

Figure 41 Critical Question about Systemic Tension

OK, now consider this. "If conflict exists between the change agent and target, then where is the real conflict?" Allow the participants to grapple with the answer until somebody guesses. "Yes, the real conflict is here (see Figure 42). If you are not aware of systemic dynamics in your organization, then countless hours will be wasted solving things at the wrong place and allowing the real issues to remain."

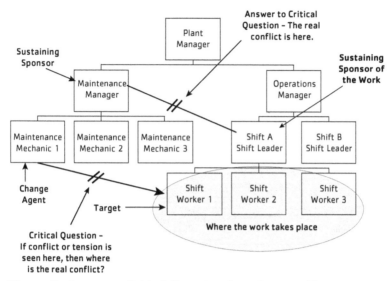

Figure 42 *Answer to Critical Question about Systemic Tension*

In actuality, alignment could be out in many places. Figure 43 shows the most likely areas of misalignment.

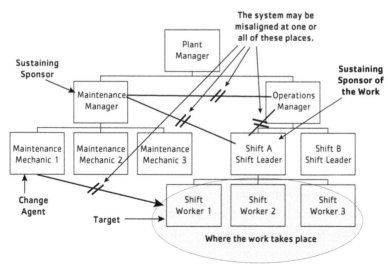

Figure 43 *Potential Misaligned Areas of the Organization*

I then complete the remaining SATA roles up to the Initiating Sponsor. I say something like, "If the maintenance mechanic cannot get work done with the target, then what they must say is *'there must be some mistake, I thought I was supposed to work with you today to get this done. OK, I will discuss priorities with your boss.'* To be clear, *this is not a conversation to get people in trouble. The purpose is to align the whole system to ensure the correct work is accomplished.* The maintenance mechanic has options, such as talking to his boss or the shift leader. The critical thing is to align the whole system.

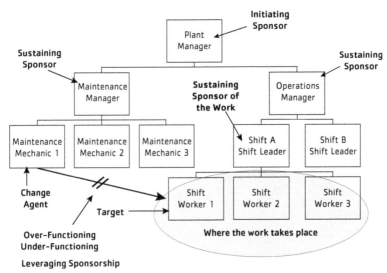

Figure 44 Flip Chart with Defined SATA Roles

If the boss of the maintenance person and shift worker disagree, then they cannot solve it at their level. In fact, they must raise it up or risk that the decision will be made by a 'test of wills' rather than what is best for the organization. Eventually it may be the maintenance manager and operations manager meeting with the plant manager, who, by definition, is the Initiating Sponsor. That is right, *the single person above all involved in the scenario is the **Initiating Sponsor** whether they realize it or not.* In fact, in many situations Initiating Sponsors do not know they are in that role, yet the system is working so there is no problem. This is another core principle: *Only worry about SATA if work is not getting accomplished.* If your organization is working well and you are getting world-class results, then there are no problems. If not, please think systemically first, especially when there is tension.

The final concept is *the black hole of sponsorship*. It happens when a high-level leader tries to create change many levels below them without aligning the whole system."

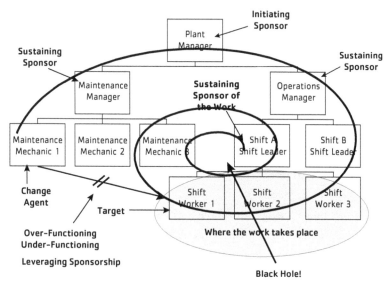

Figure 45 Black Hole of Sponsorship

I add the black hole to the flip chart at the end since it obscures the image. I then recap the SATA principles on a separate flip chart.

Four Keys to SATA

- Know your SATA role in all situations.
- Assume resistance is a systemic rather than a personality conflict.
- Solve issues at the lowest level.
- Use SATA as *an analysis tool* to find the current situation and strategize for success.

I then have the group talk to the person next to them about what they are learning. The questions are as follows:

- What are you learning?
- How does it relate to you?
- Are you confused about anything?
- Do you think you disagree with anything?

I give them several minutes to reflect and eventually bring them back to a whole group dialogue by saying, "What comments or questions do you have?" Then we dialogue about the theory and what they are learning. My dialogue varies per conversation. However, the key to helping is that you 1) fully understand SATA, 2) read my book *SOA*, 3) explore your issues with authority, and 4) help the group get as clear as possible.

Step 6: Apply Theory to Charts Written in Step 2. Give the following instructions.

Write on a flip chart (or have it already written).

Task 2—Identify SATA roles on your chart.

Go back to the chart you made earlier and:

- Circle any trouble areas.
- Rate yourself in the key role you play, and rate a key Sponsor in the circled areas.
- Build a strategy to increase the success of your problem, task, project, or initiative.

At this point I walk around the room and help participants that are struggling to accurately identify SATA roles on their charts and think through systemic conversations to help improve what they charted.

Conclusion

Sponsor/Agent/Target/Advocate is a powerful tool to help organizations align to whatever they are trying to achieve. Use it as *an analysis tool* and *not* as a program. This appendix explains exactly how I present this theory. This process takes time. I can easily spend four hours presenting this appendix without adding decision clarity of other theories. Yet, I often do a shortcut during a key activity as shown in Figure 26, Chapter 5. Use this appendix as a guide to be applied in multiple ways.

APPENDIX H

Action Substep Form

The following outline helps reduce large actions into discrete tasks to effectively track progress and allow for quick course corrections as needed.

Group: _____

Action #: _____

SPA: _____

Completion Date (By-When): _____

Write Action Item Name (example: Install four new lights over station 6):

Write Action Steps/SPA/By-When (Example: Order lights from vendor/ SPA: Joe/By-When: 12/10/18)

Step 1 _____

Step 2 _____

Step 3 _____

Step 4 _____

Step 5 _____

Intended Outcome: What is the expected outcome? How will it be measured (if applicable)?

Communication Plan: How will you inform, in advance, the people who will be impacted by this action (if applicable)?

APPENDIX I

SATA Role of Project Manager and Task SPAs

The following SATA roles were created while working with a research and design group to clarify the qualities and behaviors essential for a successful project manager and employees assigned action items (SPA) on the project.

The goal was to work in accordance with SATA to align the organization to their projects and ensure success. Written for large cross-functional, mission-critical projects, these principles can and should be adjusted to any size organization.

Project Manager SATA Role

1. Sponsored to spend enough time to interact with all people involved in the project.
2. Sufficiently knowledgeable of the project's technical aspects to communicate intelligently.
3. Knowledgeable of the *socio-technical* aspects of the workplace to drive decision clarity, single point of accountability, roles, lines of authority, and completion dates.
4. Understand and *use their personal authority* to state opinions in the face of contrary views while valuing diversity.
5. Possess the interpersonal skills to connect with people and achieve effective communication even in conflict situations.
6. Encourage the continual involvement of the workforce and support an action research approach toward constantly improving project plans and steps.
7. Monitor and **work** the timeline and decision matrix. This means problem solving with people who have actions, checking for clarity, updating the timeline, adding actions (if the timeline is in a computer, the project manager must update all involved when changes happen), informing people, educating sponsors, and immediately confronting issues. *This is not a passive role.*
8. Actively identify and communicate if the project is on track, meeting milestones, or due dates are slipping.
9. If the project is slipping, then refocus the people with tasks or sponsors to get back on track.
10. Attend to the continual education of the sponsors about the needs of the project.
11. Understand that they are *not* the boss. Persuading, coaxing, or convincing means that they are overfunctioning and probably stimulating resistance. Rather, they need to alert the appropriate sponsor(s) to clarify issues and regain direction.

Action Item (SPA) SATA Role

1. Successfully complete the action and consistently communicate with the project manager.
2. Continually update the project manager regarding time frame to complete actions as the due date approaches. This update is critical especially if an action is falling behind.
3. Negotiate time and resources necessary to complete the task by projected completion date with your own boss (i.e., educating your sponsor). Resource and time negotiation does not happen with the project manager.
4. Inform the boss if a) the action is falling behind schedule and need more time/resources and b) if it is being completed early and, therefore, you are available for other tasks.
5. Inform the project manager if the boss is unwilling to provide resources or time to complete the tasks.
6. Break down large tasks into substeps, and give those to the project manager to update the master timeline. This process provides a more accurate picture of the project scope and resource demands and helps monitor actions and progress to completion.
7. Provide reasons *if* the action will not be completed *or* has been determined as unnecessary for successful project completion.
8. ***This is not a passive role***. Many actions are linked to other events and require constant communication. Do not hesitate to act or raise issues if you are not getting what you need to complete your action.
9. Immediately raise issues to ensure task completion.

Bibliography

Bowen, M., and M. E. Kerr. 1988. *Family Evaluation.* New York, NY: W. W. Norton & Company.

Crosby, C. P. 2017. *Strategic Organizational Alignment.* New York, NY: Business Expert Press, LLC.

Crosby, G. L. 2015. *Fight, Flight, Freeze.* Seattle, WA: CrosbyOD Publishing.

Crosby, G. L. 2017. *Leadership Can Be Learned.* New York, NY. CRC Press, Taylor & Francis Group, Productivity Press.

Crosby, R. P. 2011. *Culture Change in Organizations.* Seattle, WA: CrosbyOD Publishing.

Crosby, R. P. 2015. *The Cross-Functional Workplace.* Seattle, WA: CrosbyOD Publishing.

Crosby, R. P. 2006. *Get Unstuck from Fundamentalism.* Seattle, WA: Vivo Publishing Co., Inc.

Friedman, E. 1985. *Generation to Generation.* New York, NY: Guilford Press.

Gallup Inc. 2017. *State of the American Workplace.* Washington, D.C.

Jung, C., & Lippitt, R. Study of Change as a Concept in Research Utilization. *Theory into Practice.* Feb. 1966, 5(1) 25-29. Published by the College of Education, Ohio State University.)

Lewin, K. 1997. *Resolving Social Conflicts & Field Theory in Social Science.* Washington, D.C.: American Psychological Associates.

Lippitt, G., and R. Lippitt. 1986. *The Consulting Process in Action,* 2nd ed. San Diego, CA: University Associates.

Merrill, D. W., and R. H. Reid. 1981. *Personal Style and Effective Performance.* Radner, PA: Chilton.

Minuchin, S. 1974. *Families and Family Therapy.* Cambridge, MA: Harvard University Press.

Rogers, C. 1951. *Client-Centered Therapy.* Boston, MA: Houghton Mifflin.

Schmuck, R. A., S. E. Bell, and W. E. Bell. 2012. *The Handbook of Organization Development in Schools and Colleges.* Santa Cruz, CA: Exchange Point International.

Walton, R. E. 1987. *Managing Conflict.* Reading, MA: Addison-Wesley Publishing Company, Inc.

Whitaker, C. A., and W. M. Bumberry. 1988. *Dancing with the Family.* New York, NY: Brunner/Mazel Publishers.

Whitaker, C. A., and A. Y. Napier. 1978. *The Family Crucible.* New York, NY: Harper & Row.

Williamson, D. 1991. *The Intimacy Paradox.* New York, NY: Guilford Press.

About the Author

Chris Crosby began his organization development career in 1993. He combines a business-results focus with applied behavior science and group process to help engage your employees to achieve greater results. His work spans public, private, and nonprofit industries across five continents. He is an expert in designing small and large experiential activities to solve various challenges, including mergers, large cross-functional projects, and whole-system transformations.

Chapter Index

APPENDIX INDEX

OTHER TITLES IN THE STRATEGIC MANAGEMENT COLLECTION

John A. Pearce II, Villanova University, *Editor*

- *First and Fast: Outpace Your Competitors, Lead Your Markets, and Accelerate Growth* by Stuart Cross
- *Strategies for University Management* by J. Mark Munoz and Neal King
- *Strategies for University Management, Volume II* by J. Mark Munoz and Neal King
- *Strategic Organizational Alignment: Authority, Power, Results* by Chris Crosby
- *Business Strategy in the Artificial Intelligence Economy* by J. Mark Munoz and Al Naqvi

Announcing the Business Expert Press Digital Library

Concise e-books business students need for classroom and research

This book can also be purchased in an e-book collection by your library as

- a one-time purchase,
- that is owned forever,
- allows for simultaneous readers,
- has no restrictions on printing, and
- can be downloaded as PDFs from within the library community.

Our digital library collections are a great solution to beat the rising cost of textbooks. E-books can be loaded into their course management systems or onto students' e-book readers.

The **Business Expert Press** digital libraries are very affordable, with no obligation to buy in future years. For more information, please visit **www.businessexpertpress.com/librarians**. To set up a trial in the United States, please email **sales@businessexpertpress.com**.